ARE YOU
Serious?

Also by Lee Siegel

Falling Upwards: Essays in Defense of the Imagination

Not Remotely Controlled: Notes on Television

Against the Machine: Being Human in the Age of the Electronic Mob

ARE YOU
Serious?

How to Be True and Get Real in the Age of Silly

LEE SIEGEL

HARPER

An Imprint of HarperCollins*Publishers*
www.harpercollins.com

HarperCollins books may be purchased for educational, business, or sales promotional use. For information, please write: Special Markets Department, HarperCollins Publishers, 10 East 53rd Street, New York, NY 10022.

Grateful acknowledgment is made for permission to reproduce the following:

"Dover Beach" from *Dover Beach and Other Poems* by Matthew Arnold. Reprinted by permission of Dover Publications.

"America" from *Collected Poems 1947–1980* by Allen Ginsberg. Copyright © 1956, 1959 by Allen Ginsberg. Reprinted by permission of HarperCollins Publishers.

"America" from *Collected Poems: 1947–1997* by Allen Ginsberg. Copyright © 2006 by Allen Ginsberg, LLC, used throughout the UK and Commonwealth with permission of the Wylie Agency, LLC.

Frontispiece copyright © The Estate of Max Beerbohm by permission of Berlin Associates Ltd.

FIRST EDITION

Library of Congress Cataloging-in-Publication Data
    Siegel, Lee, 1957–
        Are you serious? : how to be true and get real in the age of silly / Lee Siegel.—1st ed.
            p.   cm.
        Summary: "Are you serious? Do you know anyone who is? Cultural critic Lee Siegel combines a slashing critique of modern lightness and frivolity with a guide to being serious in an unserious age"—Provided by publisher.
        ISBN 978-0-06-176603-9 (hardback)
        1. Culture—21st century. 2. Meaning (Psychology) 3. United States—Social life and customs—21st century. I. Title.
    HM621.S526   2011
    306.09'051—dc22   2011006801

11 12 13 14 15   OV/RRD   10 9 8 7 6 5 4 3 2 1

For Julian and Harper

*Whatsoever thy hand findeth to do,
do it with thy might.*
—ECCLESIASTES 9:10

*You don't have to cook fancy or complicated
masterpieces—just good food from fresh ingredients.*
—JULIA CHILD

Let's have some new clichés.
—SAMUEL GOLDWYN

Contents

ARE YOU
Serious?

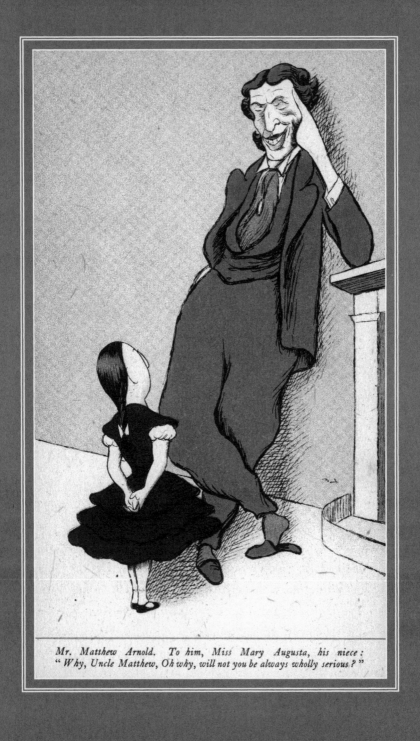

Mr. Matthew Arnold. To him, Miss Mary Augusta, his niece: "Why, Uncle Matthew, Oh why, will not you be always wholly serious?"

Overture

Are you serious?

Are you sure?

How can you tell?

In 1904, the British humorist Max Beerbohm published a cartoon about his distinguished countryman, the poet and social critic Matthew Arnold. It depicts the renowned literary man leaning against a mantelpiece, one leg crossed in front of the other. Standing before him, her braid tied with a white bow, and attired in a red pinafore dress, is his tiny niece, Mary Augusta. She is looking up at her famous uncle. Arnold is wearing house slippers and has lifted his right foot up at the toes so that the rest of his foot lolls, mischievously, out of the slipper. He is smiling mischievously, too, with amusement and a hint of derision as he listens to the young girl. The caption has her asking: "Why, Uncle Matthew, Oh why, will not you be always wholly serious?"

The meaning conveyed by Beerbohm's satire is part of the

story told by this book. But before we can understand Beerbohm's cartoon, we have to understand Arnold's idea of what he called "high seriousness."

Matthew Arnold was considered one of the wise men of his age. In essays and books that he published throughout the latter half of the nineteenth century, Arnold established his authority by developing a single powerful insight. Understanding that religion was under siege by Darwinist ideas and the forces of science and technology, Arnold prescribed a substitute for the waning faith in God. He called it "high seriousness." Seriousness, Arnold believed, was the modern person's soulfulness.

Just as the church had been the seat of faith, Arnold located "high seriousness" in culture, poetry in particular. For Arnold, poetry was the supreme aesthetic achievement, and the "essential condition," he wrote, for "supreme poetical success . . . [was] high seriousness." He was nevertheless pretty vague about what high seriousness consisted of, saying only that it had to be a "criticism of life." But Arnold's readers, steeped in religion and pained by its decline, knew exactly what he meant. They understood that high seriousness was the secular equivalent of religious belief.

This moral perspective was what Arnold meant by "criticism of life." He was thinking of the content and tone of the Bible. He might have had in mind Paul's lines in the First Letter to the Corinthians: "When I was a child, I spake as a child, I understood as a child, I thought as a child: but when I became a man, I put away childish things. For now we see through a glass, darkly; but then face to face." The idea that, spiritually, adulthood is an incomplete phase of human development is a criticism of the way the worldly pressures of self-interest and practical necessity may cloud our perception of the truth. In Arnold's eyes, literature attained high seriousness when it offered just such sensitivity to the ways life fell short of its potential fullness. And like religious sentiment, high seriousness had to be expressed with what Arnold called "absolute sincerity." Seriousness implied a trustworthy personality, just as faith in God once implied a trustworthy soul.

Arnold's conversion of religious sentiment into culture and taste held a special appeal for Americans. The high seriousness of high culture was just right for a country that lacked the rich artistic and intellectual heritage of Europe and frowned on impractical conceptualizing. Reading Arnold made the American businessman feel elevated; it inspired the American artist and intellectual to feel less alienated. Most consequential of all, Arnold's belief in art's salutary effect on morality was just right for a country whose exuberant capitalism, unrestrained by custom or convention, was—along with science and technology—wearing away the influence of religion.

Yet Arnold had nothing to say about seriousness in life. For him it abided only in culture. He made no room for the ultimate seriousness of the firefighter or the policeman, for the seriousness of the doctor, scientist, parent, teacher, friend, or lover. Nor did he embrace the seriousness of practical matters. I wonder what Arnold would have made of one contemporary businessman saying to another about a third man, "He's a serious guy." By that, the businessman means the man he is referring to is someone absolutely sincere about satisfying the interests of the people he does business with, or about sticking to his word, or about following through on what he sets out to do.

None of the forms of seriousness that are found in everyday existence has anything to do with high culture. But they are serious nonetheless.

There is another deficiency in Arnold's exaltation of high seriousness. He left out the importance of levity. Arnold's exclusion of wit or fun as an essential element of seriousness is what Beerbohm was getting at in his shrewd little cartoon. Beerbohm regarded Arnold as, in fact, more serious than the latter's solemn notion of high seriousness let on. In Beerbohm's depiction, Arnold's seriousness itself drew its power and sincerity from inner reserves of irony and mischief. Without the leavening presence of wit, Beerbohm seems to be saying, seriousness is merely the performance of seriousness. Only a child would be silly enough to expect seriousness to be "always wholly serious."

But Beerbohm was expressing something even more important. Don DeLillo captures it well in his 2010 novel, *Point Omega*. "Why is it so hard to be serious," asks one of the novel's characters, "so easy to be too serious?" Beerbohm recognized that there exists a point at which seriousness stales and needs to be refreshed by new experiences and new insights. There comes a moment when what is considered serious by culture and society has to give way to a new seriousness or it tips over into a caricature of itself. The harder it becomes to be serious, the easier it is "to be too serious." Seriousness then declines into the silly impersonation of seriousness.

Which brings us to our contemporary American life. Like Arnold's fellow Victorians, we also yearn for the ballast that religion once provided. But instead of religious faith, we now say that we are searching for *meaning*. In our daily lives, being serious is the equivalent of living meaningfully.

It is extraordinary how frequently the words "serious" and "unserious" are now used as moral categories. Serious and unserious have become the critical antipodes by which we navigate through our days: "serious" is the highest praise, "unserious" the worst insult. President Obama was elected, even by people who did not share his political values, because he was widely believed to be a "serious" person who honestly addressed the bare facts. "I supported Obama because I thought he was a serious man," declared the conservative writer Christopher Buckley. Under the headline "A Hero for Our Time," an absolutely sincere Garrison Keillor wrote in the *Los Angeles Times* that during Obama's campaign Americans realized that "we were done with the flummery and balloon juice, and the country saw its new president: a serious man for serious times." The eloquent Obama himself sometimes displayed his seriousness in Arnoldian fashion, using it to express a criticism of life in old-fashioned religious terms. "We remain a young nation," he said in his inaugural address, "but in the words of Scripture, the time has come to set aside childish things." His detractors use the same criterion to evaluate him. "He was not serious," declared Peggy Noonan about Obama's January 2011 State of the Union speech. The *Columbus Dispatch* likewise pronounced the speech "breathtakingly unserious."

Yet the very frequency with which the word "serious" is used bespeaks a confusion about just what it means. We used to know—or at least we thought we knew—who and what was serious. Talk about right and wrong was serious. Religion was serious. Intellectual debate was serious. Statesmen were serious, and journalists were serious, and novelists were serious people who often publicly commented on serious matters. And we were still surrounded by the immortal tales of timeless seriousness. Samson and Delilah! Joan of Arc! Horatio at the bridge! To this day, we are thrilled when we find the old stories reflected in instances of contemporary seriousness. The heroes of 9/11 were serious. We know that cops and firefighters are always deeply serious people in their moments of risk-taking and self-sacrifice, and we celebrate such people because we are grateful that they exist. But we also celebrate them because, just like the moral exemplars of earlier times, our contemporary heroes represent a pure, straightforward seriousness about what is at stake at every moment in life. They remind us of the naked urgency that runs without cease through our allotted hours of mortal time.

Nowadays, however, we live in the aftermath of decades of public exposure of private foibles. We have inherited disenchantment with authority in all realms of American life. We are surrounded by irony, arrogant informality, and the most outrageous irreverence as official, public styles. This makes us both yearn for seriousness and mistrust it when we think we might have found it. Some commentators were quick to point out that Obama's reference to the necessity of putting aside childish things and growing up had misrepresented the original sentiment. Paul was saying that just as childhood had to be completed by adulthood, so too did growing up have to be completed by a spiritual awakening. Until then, even as adults, we see "through a glass, darkly." Suddenly, Obama's indisputable seriousness seemed like an unserious appropriation of a serious statement about existence. The question arises: Which was more serious? Obama's attempt to be serious? Or the mistrust that greeted it?

The more we wish to be serious and to find seriousness, it seems, the more we lose sight of what seriousness really is. On these occasions, we are like little Mary Augusta, imploring the people around us to be "always wholly serious" because we have forgotten just how witty, fresh, and strange true seriousness can be. As a result, we too easily fall prey to the mere performance of seriousness—to its caricature. The performance of seriousness—from politics to journalism to literary and intellectual life—has become the quintessential American silliness. Take, for example, the talk show demagogues of our day, from Left to Right, whose extremist antics occur behind the facade of the most extreme seriousness.

Yet for all the dizzying ubiquity of the word "serious," and for all the crazy variety of what passes for seriousness, we know when we are being serious, and we know seriousness when we encounter it.

Or do we?

Consider this book a guide to seriousness past and present, as well as a survivor's manual for the seriousness-starved. It is about what Arnold might have meant by seriousness, but also about seriousness in our everyday lives, and about those other realms of seriousness and serious anti-seriousness, hinted at by Beerbohm, in all their permutations and humble realities. What follows is a serious (of course it is) exploration of one of life's most elusive yet essential qualities. Someone who loved Italy said once that the Italians were too Italian, but everyone else was not Italian enough. Seriousness is like that, too. *Why, oh why can we not be always wholly serious?* There is a silly answer to that question, and a serious one. Let's see what they are.

CHAPTER ONE

The Urge to Be Serious

How Seriousness Is Used

Only in America could reality become a trend, as in "reality television." But then, only in America do we take time out for a "reality check," as if anyone so far gone as to lose their sense of reality would actually know what to check in order to get it back. I mean, get real. Of course, only in America could the admonishment "get real" be a reproach, and "unreality" be a sin.

Now that we're on the subject, only in America do we say "I mean" before we say what we mean, as if it were an acceptable convention for people to go around saying what they didn't mean, and it had become another convention to make the distinction, before saying anything of consequence, between meaning and not meaning what you are about to say.

Already I'm, like, getting dizzy. Which raises the question of why Americans distance themselves from what they are saying by putting "like" before the description of something, as if people are nervous about committing to a particular version of reality, or to a direct, unmediated, nonmetaphorical experience of the real.

In a society like ours where reality is so slippery that we actually now have a whole branch of entertainment explicitly claiming to depict it, the urge to be serious is very powerful. I don't know exactly when the words "serious" and "seriously" began to perform the function of an intensifier. But using them that way speaks volumes about our yearning to be serious.

That is a seriously beautiful sunset. That girl is seriously hot. That is a serious CD collection. Those are some serious abs. My favorite is, He is seriously funny. Meaning: Not what passes for funny. But truly, authentically, honestly, originally funny. Seriously funny. So much of the life around us has been seized by advertising and Hollywood, so much of our experience has been caricatured and "branded," that we use the word "serious" in an attempt to reclaim experience for ourselves. It's a way to distinguish the originality of something from all the many imitations and copies of the thing.

When we say, "That is a serious hamburger," we mean that it is not like all the hamburgers we have seen in ads and commercials. It is not the proverbial hamburger of childhood outings with Dad, or of stoned, late-night, teenaged visits to McDonald's, White Castle, or that Greek diner. No, "that is a serious hamburger" means that is a true hamburger, unlike any imitation or copy. It means, At last! I am having a fresh, original experience of a hamburger that exists in fullness of being beyond all the cheap replicas of a burger. Likewise, serious money means not the tired, trite, wearyingly familiar image of money. Serious money is life-changing, status-transforming, "I'll never have to work again" money. It is not simply a thing to be possessed. It occupies its own category of being. The $7 billion that Facebook founder Mark Zuckerberg is worth qualifies as serious money. Barack Obama, with his millions in book royalties, does not have serious money.

My dictionary traces the etymology of "serious" back to an Old English word meaning "heavy" or "sad." I have my own fanciful origin of the term. I like to think that the word is somehow tangled up with the Spanish verb *ser*. *Ser* means "to be" in Spanish, but it is distinct from the Spanish verb *estar*, which also means "to be." You use *estar* to describe a mood or an emotion. You use *ser* to describe identity or the particular traits that make up the essence of a person. *Estar* implies temporariness; *ser* connotes permanence. In that sense, "serious" is a state of being in which you are fully aware of who you are, and what your place is in the world at that moment. You are also aware of who someone else is, and what their precise relationship is to you. That is what you expect when you are told that someone is "serious"; that what he or she does will follow from who he or she is. We spend our days floating along on a train of disconnected feelings and moods, waiting for the moment when we suddenly become aware of the connection between who we are and what we are doing.

You might say that *estar* is an artificial state of being because it is contingent on the forces that create our moods and cause them to change. *Ser*, on the other hand, is wholly natural. It is how we live in clarity and conscientiousness. *Ser* is organic seriousness. When people say that they are searching for meaning, they are saying that they are trying to find something serious about which they can be serious. To live meaningfully is to live seriously.

I know what some of you are thinking. This guy is making too much of a hamburger. Siegel is being too serious. In fact, the attraction and the aversion to being serious is a pendular American motion, as we shall see in a later chapter. A constant fear runs through American life, that you are either too serious—and thus depressed, in the Old English sense of the word—or not serious enough. As Abraham Lincoln, one of the most serious people who ever lived, wrote to a woman he was courting:

> *I have commenced two letters to send you before this, both of which displeased me before I got half done, and so I tore them up. The first I thought wasn't serious enough, and the second was on the other extreme.*

As we've noted, in contemporary American life, "serious" seems to be used more frequently the less its meaning is clear. "Serious" occurs in the most diverse and contradictory contexts. It has traveled far from Arnold's snobbish use of the term, and even beyond Beerbohm's realms of laughter and absurdity. Yet the impulse behind the use of the word—the desire to be serious!—remains constant.

"If you wanna be taken seriously, you gotta have *serious hair*," Melanie Griffith says in the movie *Working Girl*. She turns out to be right, though neither highfalutin' Matthew Arnold nor mischievous Max Beerbohm would have had any idea what she was talking about. In *The Godfather*, Don Corleone tells Virgil Sollozzo, a gangster newly arrived in town who has joined up with a rival crime family, that he has agreed to meet with him because he has heard that Sollozzo is a "serious man." The don means that Sollozzo means what he says, but Sollozzo is also serious in another sense: he ends up nearly killing the don and murdering one of his sons. You might say that Sollozzo turned out to be too serious, while Don Corleone was not serious enough.

Even exemplars of Arnoldian high seriousness are of no help in clarifying what "serious" truly signifies. Arnold's foremost American disciple was the literary critic Lionel Trilling. What fun Beerbohm might have had with him. About sixty years ago, Trilling offered a provocative insight into the social construction of seriousness. "It might be said," he wrote, "that our present definition of a serious book is one which holds before us some image of society to consider and condemn." In other words, Trilling scorned what he regarded as the "middlebrow" notion of seriousness. For Trilling and other intellectuals of his time, "middlebrow" meant art—or taste in art—that pretended to value difficulty and complexity but settled instead for easy sentiments and simple ideas. In Trilling's eyes, social outrage was an instantly available emotion that provided the appearance of a complex, critical attitude toward society, and so it often served as the quickest route to "seriousness."

Trilling was thinking of—to use his mildly ironic phrase—"commercially successful serious novels," like those of John Steinbeck, James Gould Cozzens, and James Jones. We don't have much socially conscious commercial fiction anymore. Rather, Hollywood has taken on the function of holding "before us some image of society to consider and condemn." Think of the award for Best Picture, bestowed upon the film considered to be the most serious of the past year. The last five movies, as of this writing, to have won the award are: *Crash* (2005), a movie about racial and ethnic prejudice; *The Departed* (2006), a movie about police corruption; *No Country for Old Men* (2007), a movie about the way violence, greed, and sheer chance expose the sham of social harmony; *Slumdog Millionaire* (2008), a movie about the rottenness at the heart of capitalism; and *The Hurt Locker* (2009), a movie about the sickness of war.

But was Trilling right? Are these movies pretending to be serious by taking up "serious" themes that are actually emotionally and intellectually facile? Or was Trilling, like so many other elite intellectuals, a seriousness snob who felt the periodic urge to renounce his own serious nature when he found it reflected in contexts that were unfamiliar and even inhospitable to his own?

The meaning of "seriousness" is seriously elusive. We spend our days searching for a way to be serious. We exhort our children to be serious. We look for serious people to associate with, to befriend, to fall in love with. We search for serious work. We get tired of all the buying and selling, of all the numbing routines that fill our days and consume our time, tired of the petty but necessary white lies that we have to tell and endure being told. We want to feel that there is a purpose to our lives. We want to feel that our experiences add up to something that *explains* our experiences. We wish to stop thinking about our self-interest, just for a minute, and get caught up in something larger than ourselves. We want to be serious.

Yet we don't want the busy, transactional, ego-gratifying world to pass us by. We do not want to get weighed down by lugubrious seriousness, by the Old English origin of the word. Maybe that's why "serious business" has become such a universal expression. It captures our ambivalence about being serious. Serious business is not just business as usual. It's fresher and more original and more consequential than that. At the same time, it's not so out of the ordinary that it takes us away from the importance of attending to our business.

Still, for all our ambivalence and confusion about how to be serious, and in what degree, our yearning to be serious persists. It makes its way into our speech again and again.

"Serious" as an intensifier is as ubiquitous, if you will pardon my crudity, as the word "fucking." The two terms are like the respectable and the unrespectable sides of the same social coin. We may say, for example, that something is "fucking great" or that something is "seriously great." "Fucking great" means that there is something asocial about the thing that is great, or at least something asocial about the way we think about the thing. It could lead us into turbulent waters. "Seriously great" means that no matter how great it is, it will remain within the bounds of what is normal and acceptable.

The modulations are infinite. "I'm seriously upset with you" means that you are upset in a way that cannot be captured by all the many representations of being upset that we have been flooded with throughout our lives. You are "seriously" upset; you are upset in an unprecedented way. You are also upset in a way that has purpose, attention, and continuity. That is to say, there are going to be consequences to your being upset. You are going to stay focused on being upset. You are going to follow through on being upset. But being "seriously" upset means that you are sticking to the rules. You are not going to be hurtful. You are not going to do anything reckless. If you are "fucking upset," on the other hand, then all bets are off. The still-taboo word is out of social bounds. It means that you are probably going to do something that is equally out of bounds. You might be reckless. You might hurt someone.

Use of the intensifier "seriously" puts the brakes on a situation where "fucking" might be used instead. He is a "fucking womanizer" expresses disgust and disapproval. He is a "serious womanizer" is an emphatic description that indicates moral neutrality and even a hint of admiration. "Serious" as an intensifier brings a situation right up to the brink of emergency and violence without crossing the line.

But by the same token, "fucking" is so commonly understood to be an expression of power used by someone who feels powerless that "serious" has a sincerity "fucking" lacks. All a cop needs to say is that you are in "serious" trouble. If he says you are in "fucking" trouble, you might wonder about his state of mind. After all, cops are at their most serious when they are wordlessly arresting someone. The same goes for "We're in some serious shit." The world is brimming with shit and with people who say "shit." But serious shit—ah, that's the real thing. It's shit with official consequences. We add "serious" to an expletive when we want to preserve the outlaw force of it while shedding its implication of impotence. "Serious" as an intensifier makes something both respectable and absolutely urgent.

Or as Group Home raps: "Me and my fam, take this rap shit serious / New York to L.A., and you niggaz best to fear this."

Interlude: The Serious Business of Numbers

Between the previous section and this one, I had the urge to snack on some cheese, but I resisted the impulse because my cholesterol is a combined 205 and it should be less than 200. The LCD, or bad cholesterol, is on the high side, coming in at about 135. It's supposed to be less than 130. The HCD, or good cholesterol, is 52. It should be above 40. My father's father, my father, my maternal grandfather, and my maternal grandmother all died of heart attacks. That means that I have a 1 in 50 chance of succumbing to the same illness. On the other hand, I don't smoke, so that lowers the chance to 1 in 200. I used to drink between 3 and 4 glasses of wine a night—the maximum healthy amount for men is 2 glasses per day, while for women it's one.

I don't drink alcohol at all anymore, except on the rare occasions I go out to socialize. Then I have between 4 and 6 glasses of wine. If I go out once a week, that is well under the recommendation of 14 glasses per week for men. Twice a week brings me to between 8 and 12 glasses, which is still just below the limit. But I don't go out much because I'm trying to finish this book. It's 3 months overdue. I was given 18 months to write it. It should be 50,000 words long. At 250 words a page, that's about 200 pages. I'm writing approximately 1,000 words a day. At that rate, I should be finished in about 50 days. The thing is, I don't always write on weekends. Say I'll be done in 60 days, to be on the safe side.

Some days, I admit, I don't hit 1,000 words. Yesterday I was on the phone for several hours with an old, dear friend who is pregnant. She's 40, which means that she has a 1 in 100 chance of having a baby with Down syndrome. So far, she's had two diagnostic tests. The first test determined that she actually had a 1/800 chance of having an "affected" baby, as the clinical euphemism goes. Her AFP level was 1.2, her HPP was 1.0, and her PPP was .98. This was very good, because all three levels are supposed to be around 1.0. The false negative rate is 5 percent. The second test had less encouraging results, putting her risk factor at 1 in 100. The second test has a false positive rate of up to 20 percent. This result made my friend think that she should get an amniocentesis, an invasive procedure that extracts a small amount of amniotic fluid to test for an affected baby. This test has an accuracy rate of 99.7 percent. It holds a risk of miscarriage of between 1 in 200 and 1 in 1,600. My friend is weighing the possibility of having an affected baby—somewhere between 1 in 100 and 1 in 800, not counting the high possibility of a 20 percent false positive from the second test—against the risk of miscarriage: again, between 1 in 200 and 1 in 1,600. The only experience I could draw from to try to advise her was the time, for one reason or another, a doctor recommended that I get a full-body CT scan. This test has a 1 in 100,000 chance of causing a fatal result. I declined. It then turned out that I had experienced a false alarm. These happen at about a rate of 1 in 125 every year.

I told my friend that she should ask her ob-gyn what to do, but she told me that he was so cautious that he simply presented her with lots of data without offering any kind of guidance, or even subjective opinion. Apparently, 1 out of every 62 ob-gyns will get sued by a patient in the course of his career. That accounts for his caution. His malpractice insurance has shot up over 150 percent in the last 10 years. My friend understands his situation. What concerns her is that he was once included in *New York* magazine's list of the 10 best ob-gyns in New York, but he didn't make the list this year. I told her that was one thing she shouldn't worry about. I knew with between 94 and 96 percent certainty that the list is compiled by 6 editors, 2 of whom were spending just one-third of their time in the office working on the list. Anyway, just because her doctor didn't make it into the top 10, it didn't mean that he wasn't in the top 25, or 50, or 100. Since there were 16,428 ob-gyns in New York, even if he was in the top 500, that was still pretty good. On the other hand, someone in America is suing their doctor 2.4 times an hour.

Numbers are to seriousness what yarn is to knitting needles. They are useless without the connecting instruments of intuition and knowledge, which exist beyond mere information.[*]

---

[*] All of the aforementioned numbers are hypothetical and not to be taken seriously.

CHAPTER TWO

My Comical Struggle to Be Serious

A s an asthmatic child suffering from a variety of upper respira-
tory illnesses, I carved out my own, inevitably comical, American path toward seriousness. I made my sickbed a kingdom
of serious reading. If I wasn't laid up for a day with an asthmatic
attack, I was restricted to my bed for weeks or months with bron-
chitis or pneumonia. My stricken metabolism, slowed to a crawl,
had a healthy effect on my consciousness. Out of serious ailment
came submersion in what I feebly understood as a serious frame
of mind. At around fifteen, all through the winter, I lay swaddled
in blankets reading Leo Tolstoy's epic of the Napoleonic Wars. I
passed in and out of each one of the characters in *War and Peace*
as if in and out of different climates. I was beautiful Natasha,
eventually to be redeemed by Tolstoy into a corpulent house-

wife. I was proud, noble Prince Andrei, his all-consuming love for Natasha the only flaw in his being. Most thoroughly of all, I inhabited Nikolai Rostov, the romantic, excitable young man who rushes off to war to defend sacred Russia from the invading French hordes. When French soldiers shoot at Nikolai as he runs for his life across a bridge, he thinks to himself, "Mother! Mother! Why are they shooting at your precious little boy, whom you hug to your breast and love so much?!" Though Tolstoy meant by this scene to portray Nikolai as a romantic fool who cannot grasp the seriousness of war, it spoke to me, the sickly boy whom my mother hugged to her breast and loved so much.

How vulnerable to serious trouble a serious book had made me!

That summer I was walking along the highway just around the corner from my house with some friends, when we shouted to a couple of pretty girls coming out of a drive-in restaurant called Pizza Town. As soon as the words left our mouths, a dozen guys in their late teens poured out of two vans parked by the restaurant and walked over to us with that uncertain haste that spreads through a group steeling itself into a mob.

A street fight always starts with a push and builds from there, and the first kid they shoved was Kenny O'Shea. Kenny was a short, reticent boy, thoughtful but not very bright, sweet and good-natured. My mind was filled with ragtag romantic notions that had migrated from books, TV, and movies into my head, where they set up their troublesome operations. So, despite the fact that I felt relieved the gang had singled out Kenny instead of me, I heard myself say, "Leave him alone!" even though that was the last thing I wanted to say. In one unified motion, the gang swarmed all over me, punching and kicking me while Kenny scrambled away.

I ran in circles and zigzags as they chased me around the clearing, grabbing for my arms and my shirt. A few tough guys were holding brassy and shiny things, which I thought were brass knuckles but turned out to be doorknobs. It must have been a doorknob that crashed down just above my forehead, knocking me dizzy as blood trickled down through my hair. Then, suddenly, a tall, solid boy wearing a flannel shirt was looming a few feet away from me. I can still see the look on his face as he focused his concentration. He had the intensity of Rodin's *Thinker*. To this day, I cannot square the seriousness of his attention, the utter intellectuality of it—as though he were a Zen master considering where to plant an orchid in his garden—I cannot square that look with the flying kick he landed on my chest, busting the wind out of me and nearly making me lose consciousness.

As I lay bleeding in the dirt between the highway and a miserable sliver of woods, a voice cried inside me, "Mommy! Mommy! How could he do this to your precious little boy whom you love so much?" The very fact that a great work of literature had seemed to bear out my own experience proved to me that despite (or maybe because of) my beating, I was living a serious life.

Silly? You don't know the half of it. Before Tolstoy's *War and Peace*, there was Fyodor Dostoyevsky's *Notes from Underground*. It was yet another fateful step in the formation of a purely literary consciousness that had nothing to do with the world around me and the way people live.

Notes from Underground fell into my hands in ninth grade the way an innocent person might find himself holding a heroin-filled syringe at a party, thereby sealing his sad fate. I had been involuntarily enrolled in what was euphemistically referred to as an "enrichment program." Read: "Program designed to make boys and girls more serious." In reality, it was the official name for a *Manchurian Candidate*–like experiment in which happy-go-lucky boys and girls were whisked away from their favorite television shows into a shadowy world of triple meanings, narcotic generalizations, and ambiguous imagery. *Notes from Underground* was our first homework assignment.

What buried flaw in my being responded to this perverse Slavic sham is still a mystery to me. But all of a sudden, I started explaining to my gentle, loving parents that common sense was the collective hallucination of madmen. That the idea that two plus two equaled five was "tantamount" (a word I envisioned as a white steed rising heavenward to steadily beating drums) to a "spiritual" (another fave) rebirth.

In a word, I had become fatally serious. Arnold would have been proud. Beerbohm would have smiled.

Rationality, I informed Mom and Dad, was like a dagger in the soul. Week after week, I expounded the cult of unhappiness at the dinner table. Finally exiling myself to my room, I consoled myself with the existential philosophy of Albert Camus, who tells us that to live honestly we must ask ourselves every day whether we should take our own lives. There was no agency, on the local, state, or federal level, to intervene on my behalf. How do you do a "seriousness intervention"? The die was cast.

The Arnoldian literary critic Harold Bloom once wrote that literature's most precious gift is to teach us to be alone with ourselves. Easy to say when you're surrounded by adoring graduate students. I began to carry around my solitude like a trophy, cultivating alienation the way some of my friends lavished care on their pet gerbils. It was an unhealthy situation.

This wasn't just baffled adolescent desire rushing with relief into morbid tales of anger and renunciation. Uplifting writing derailed me, too. When, in tenth grade, Antonia Perella—the love of my hormone-addled life!—finally chose me as her partner at a square dance, I was so afraid of not rising to the occasion that I refused, ennobling my cold feet by summoning to my mind Plato's vision of love (see *Phaedrus*) as moist wings sprouting from the lover's body. I just didn't feel the wings business, I told myself. Recently, I learned from Facebook that Antonia married a professional wrestler. Talk about being serious. Have you ever tried to wriggle out of a crucifix armbar?

But even Oedipus eventually saw the light (or so Sophocles tells us—you decide). Somewhere in my freshman year of college, my mind, thankfully, began to close a little and the world started to open up. I was on the slow boat to recovery . . . and then calamity struck. A "friend" lent me his copy of Saul Bellow's *Herzog*.

If ever there was a candidate for strict congressional oversight, it is this cunning little book. Moses Herzog is a professor of Romantic literature in the full throes of midlife crisis, who writes countless letters to the famous literary and intellectual dead.

These scintillating one-sided exchanges, in which Herzog quotes and spars with the formative minds of Western civilization, made me feel that I was mastering life as I read them, just as a budding music historian might have the delusion that he was mastering the piano simply by listening to a sonata by Beethoven.

In fact, as I discovered many years later, Bellow was *joking*. What he wanted to demonstrate, in the figure of poor Herzog, was the utter ineffectuality of the most potent ideas. Thanks for letting me know, pal. Since nobody at the time bothered to let me in on all the fun, I finished *Herzog* as, well, Herzog. At job interviews, I assured prospective employers of my immunity to distraction by admiringly invoking Aristotle's observation that copulation makes all animals sad. To puzzled women on dates, I expatiated on the German thinkers Hegel and Sombart. "What's wrong?" one girl asked me as we stared into each other's eyes and I smiled ruefully. "Oh, nothing," I said. "Spinoza associated desire with disconnected thinking—that's all."

And so it went, just like that, reaching the high point of absurdity when I applied for a job at the *Social Register*, thinking that it was a socialist magazine. I had been reading Gramsci by way of Silone by way of Engels on the Manchester working class. So enthusiastic had I become about the sweeping inexorabilities of dialectical materialism that I neglected to pick up an actual, material copy of the *Social Register*. My interviewer, a pleasant fortyish man in a rumpled white shirt and tie, sat in his Fifth Avenue office and listened politely, his lip curling ever so slightly, to my reflections on hegemony, slave consciousness, and "boring from within." He even walked me to the door.

As you can see, I was a quick study in intellectual matters, but I was slow to learn about life. Well into adulthood, I believed that seriousness about culture was seriousness about life. I was half right.

When I was nineteen, I moved in with Gretchen Anderson, an aspiring painter I had met in a nineteenth-century philosophy class at the state college where we both were enrolled. I still have a book called *Essential Writings of Hegel*, on whose inside cover I carefully wrote her phone number in big, confident digits. We rented the downstairs apartment in a two-story two-family house in Passaic, New Jersey, which belonged to an elderly Italian American couple who lived on the second floor.

I was in the most intense part of that stage in my life when I identified seriousness with art and ideas. The search for seriousness had brought Gretchen and me together. It also elevated us above our lot in life: the nowhere state college where we had met and where we were still enrolled; the disheartening, unambitious atmosphere of our homes; the endless struggle to make money and keep our heads above water by trying to balance school and work. I had collected hundreds of books and we installed some of them in cheap bookshelves and stacked the rest on the floor against the walls. Our apartment was packed with books the way igloos are packed with ice.

The authors and artists I embraced were inseparable from my sense of honor. Gretchen, in contrast, spoke of her favorite artists with maternal feeling. She displayed the protectiveness toward them with which she had enveloped me. To hear her talk about the way Matisse abandoned line for color, you would have thought she was a mother describing her child's first words. She treated her copy of Paul Klee's diaries, its covers loose and its cracked spine about to break, like the Bible.

We didn't just admire the artists and thinkers of the past; we poured all our own feelings of hurt and bewilderment into them. The problem was that when we weren't discussing art and books, we had nothing to talk about.

So we fled our igloo of books in Passaic for Tromøy, a little island off the coast of Norway, where Gretchen's grandmother lived. There Gretchen would become a famous painter, and I would become an (eventually) immortal poet. That was the plan. We would immerse our relationship so completely in books and art that we would never have to worry about the nature of our relationship.

First, we flew to London and traveled by train to Newcastle, where the hulking policemen we asked for directions spoke, it seemed to me, some incomprehensible Brobdingnagian dialect. I was always thinking in literary terms. If I didn't make a literary association naturally, I forced myself to come up with one, because that was how it suited me to think of myself.

It was a late English summer. As if in a dream, we hauled our luggage—I had a Samsonite suitcase filled with about sixty pounds of books—through a fading golden light along streets rinsed dark by rain, finally boarding a bus, knocking our bags against the other riders as we self-consciously dragged them down the narrow aisle. I nearly gave myself a hernia carrying the light blue suitcase with its heavy trove of seriousness. I had to grip the handle with two hands, lean away from the suitcase for leverage, and heave it with me, swinging it from side to side as my arms grew tired.

Back in Passaic, I had explained to Gretchen that I needed the books to sustain me while writing my poems in her grandmother's house. The books gave me the pedestal of a writer's identity. They made me serious. Without them, I was a confused and lonely nineteen-year-old, looking not for adventure but for a safer home.

We spent several months in Norway and returned to Passaic, penniless, jobless, unhappy, and even more serious about our authors and artists and ideas than before. We soon parted ways. I took my books, and she took hers. Instead of seriously embracing Gretchen and her life, I had looked right past her to some lofty ideal of seriousness that had nothing to do with her, or me, or the life around us.

But, then, in fairness to my young self, I had absorbed a primary feature of American existence. Thanks to Matthew Arnold and the Victorians, we learn throughout college—for all the changes that have been made to the curriculum—to associate seriousness with the "higher" pursuits of art and intellect. It is only as we grow older that we recognize how seriousness in the course of our daily existence is even more meaningful, and even more urgent. That is when we also learn to demand more from the productions of art and intellect.

Consider the following vignettes as illustrations of seriousness in everyday life.

CHAPTER THREE

Notes Toward a Definition of Seriousness

Beatrice and Dante

Beatrice is a designer who lives in Manhattan and has her own small but successful clothing line. Dante is a lawyer working in corporate litigation. They met at a party a local gym held on its opening day and they've been together for nine years. Beatrice is thirty-seven, Dante forty. When she hit thirty, Beatrice wanted to ask Dante where it was all going, but she was afraid of driving him away. At the same time, her therapist was telling her that she could do better; Dante never told her he loved her, and he ate off her plate in restaurants. He also texted between courses. And he snored. When Beatrice was thirty-two, Dante started dropping hints about being committed to each other, but she was angry that he had waffled for so long, and anyway, she had just sold her line to a chain of upscale department stores and thought that if the sky was the limit in business, better romance was sure to follow. She told Dante that she needed space. They kept their separate apartments.

On Beatrice's thirty-fifth birthday, Dante took her to Le Bernardin, turned off his BlackBerry, didn't eat off her plate, and presented her with a little red Cartier box. She was so excited that she felt like a teenager, but she didn't care. When she opened the box and saw diamond earrings, she almost hurled them in his face. Instead, she wept and sobbed. That night he told her he loved her and they had gratifying sex. He still snored while he slept. But instead of clamping her pillow over her ears and imagining herself minutely deconstructing Dante's character to her therapist as she usually did, Beatrice rested her head against his back and sighed. For the next two years, she told herself that she had a man who was always, mostly, there for her, who was generous and kind and, mostly, trustworthy, who accepted her flaws and whose flaws she, mostly, accepted. That was more than any of her other single friends had. Plus, the lack of a clear commitment meant that the possibility of sex with other people was always hovering in the background for each of them—and each of them did, once in a while, stray secretly from the other—a sometimes anguishing touch of unknowableness and strangeness that kept their sex life, mostly, a satisfying surprise. That was more than any of Beatrice's married friends had.

When Beatrice turned thirty-seven, she passed four nannies in a row pushing small children in strollers as she walked along

Broadway on the Upper West Side. Then she tripped over a broken hump in the sidewalk. Cursing and rifling through her bag, she found her cell phone and left a message on Dante's voice mail telling him that either they got serious, or he would never see her again.

Jackson

Jackson came to New York City as a young man, right out of college, to make a life for himself as a painter. He took classes in the morning at the Art Students League, worked in the afternoons for a commercial artist in Midtown, and spent his nights painting in his small East Village studio. From time to time, he filled in for a friend who worked as a guard at the Metropolitan Museum of Art. He flung himself into the scene around him, enjoying the parties and the women. He relished the quick, intense friendships with strangers and he began, with pleasure and shame, to feel distant from his college friends. In the midst of all his fun, he felt that he was enlarging his experience, opening himself to the world. He felt that he was growing up.

Jackson applied himself to his art with furious discipline. He wouldn't rest until he had turned himself into a more than competent draftsman. He mastered color theory. He absorbed the history of Western art. He worked all night painting and reading until his mind and his hand became prehensile halves of the same detached, disembodied self—Jackson, perfected—and he fell asleep wherever he happened to be working. He was a serious artist with serious values and ambitions.

Ten years later, Jackson is living in a Westchester hamlet with a wife and two children. Though he found an obscure gallery in Brooklyn to represent him, he wasn't able to make a living as a painter. Tired of dismal part-time jobs, he gratefully accepted his former boss's offer of a full-time position at the commercial-art studio where Jackson used to work. Over the years, he became a partner in the firm. He married a schoolteacher he met while waiting for a bus in a snowstorm. They had two children and moved out of the city to Westchester.

Jackson still paints on the weekends, but he directs most of his energy to the lives of his young children, and to his wife, who began wrestling with depression after the birth of her second child coincided with the death of both her aged parents. "Everything for the *kinder*," Jackson joked to a neighbor, an insurance adjuster named Philip, the father of four kids and the type of person Jackson feels most comfortable around these days. Jackson loves guiding his children, ages four and six, toward the fulfillment of their most serious projects, even if these change by the week, and he loves helping to heal his wife (Jackson, perfected). He is a serious husband and father, with serious values and ambitions.

When Worlds of Seriousness Collide

There was once a professor at Columbia University unanimously considered a legend of seriousness. His name was Sidney Morgenbesser and he taught philosophy. He was also legendarily witty. I believe it was Morgenbesser who said that the difference between undergraduates and graduate students was that when a professor made a joke, the former laughed while the latter wrote it down. Or maybe someone else said that. Anyway, Morgenbesser was a serious man, a profoundly serious man, who was also a connoisseur of true seriousness.

Stories abound about the way Morgenbesser's particular blend of seriousness, when it took an excursion out into the world, sent crazy waves of meaning through any situation in which he happened to find himself. My favorite story involves Morgenbesser on the New York subway. He lived with his mother for much of his life and every day he took the subway from his mother's apartment in Lower Manhattan up to Columbia, at the other end of the island.

One day, late in the morning, Morgenbesser stepped onto the train, sat down, and looked around him. The car was empty. Morgenbesser took out his beloved pipe and began filling it with tobacco. The car is empty, he later reported thinking, there's no one here who might be bothered, so! I can smoke. He lit his pipe and sat back puffing. He loved the familiar ride along the city's subterranean spine.

After a few minutes, a transit cop walked into the car. He walked over to Morgenbesser and stopped in front of him. "You can't smoke in here," the cop said. Morgenbesser later reported answering, "But the car is empty, there's no one here who might be bothered, so! I can smoke." The officer of the law stared at the professor of philosophy. "What if everyone thought like you do?" he asked. Morgenbesser's profoundly serious mind made a triple swoop and landed on an obscure branch of the tree of knowledge. This was the concept known as the "categorical imperative," formulated by the eighteenth-century German philosopher Immanuel Kant. According to the categorical imperative, each man must act as though his particular action were a universal moral law. In Morgenbesser's democratic eyes, the transit cop had not instructed him to stop smoking. Rather, he had uttered one of Western culture's immortal precepts. It was time, therefore, for Morgenbesser to pay the cop the homage of one of his patented serious jokes. "What are you," the philosopher said, "a Kant?"

Intensely focused on the serious enforcement of the law, the transit cop heard, instead of the philosopher's name, a familiar unphilosophical word with similar phonetic qualities, which he instantly associated with a serious insult to his status as a guardian and enforcer of the law, and thus as an insult to the Law itself. And so, the serious police officer took the serious philosopher into custody and conveyed him to the local precinct. There Morgenbesser explained to the sergeant on duty what "a Kant" was.

When Worlds of Seriousness Collide, Part II

I was once invited by a woman friend to accompany her to a dinner party on Park Avenue, somewhere in the seventies. The host was a very wealthy banker, a Rothschild, in fact.

I happened to be sitting next to him and, after a few glasses of wine, I decided to tell him an old joke. It was a joke about a poor Jew from a Polish shtetl called Tarnopol, who schleps all the way to Paris to ask M. Rothschild to give him two hundred francs. In exchange, he says, he will reveal to M. Rothschild the secret of eternal life. It is an interminable joke. Here is the punch line: "Monsieur Rothschild, go to Tarnopol. A rich man never died there yet." The banker laughed minimally, politely. Then he returned to his food.

I performed a quick psychoanalysis on myself and concluded that I had told this unsuccessful joke because sitting next to the very wealthy banker in his palatial apartment made me feel precisely like that poor Jew from Tarnopol. Thus I had attempted to reverse the situation by making him laugh at a joke about a poor Jew who turns the tables on M. Rothschild by using wit to put wealth in its place. So much for that.

Little did I know that fate was on my side that evening.

At one point, ever gracious, my wealthy host asked me what I did. I told him that I was a writer. What sort of writer are you, he asked. Always mindful of John Updike's definition of critics as "pigs at the pastry cart"—in fact, I was literally lapping up a divine dessert—I told him that I wrote about culture. For example, he said. For example, I said, I have an essay coming out about Freud's notion of Thanatos, the death instinct. The what? he said, suddenly fixing his eyes on me. The death instinct, I repeated. The idea that everyone, I explained, on some level, wishes to die.

The wealthy banker gently laid down his fork and turned toward me. Everyone wants on some level to die? he said. That's ridiculous. Who said that again? he asked. Freud did, I said. Well, he said, he's wrong, and that's nonsense. No one wants to die, he said. He looked me in the eye and said it again, No one wants to die. Well, I said, seizing the advantage, that's what Freud said. Incidentally, I added, it is a famous and powerful concept in the history of Western civilization. We returned to our dessert. He seemed to be brooding. After a few minutes, he turned impulsively toward me and said, Do you know what I like to do on the weekends? I like to hunt grouse. I shoot them by the dozens. He raised his arms. Boom, boom, boom, he said. Like that. Boom, boom, boom. He was graciously, quietly furious about demonstrating that not only did he not want to die, but that he rained death himself when he so desired.

For a fleeting nanosecond, the power of serious reflection, in the form of an idea, met the power of serious material doing, in the form of creating wealth.

One Evening in Hyde Park

A woman I know—let's call her Sarah—attended the University of Chicago as an undergraduate. The school's renowned dedication to seriousness was what had attracted her. The Great Books, a set of fifty-four volumes that contain the most serious writings of Western civilization, had been the brainchild of Robert Maynard Hutchins, a fabled early president of the university.

Sarah took up comparative literature as a major. She lived in a rundown apartment in Hyde Park with one roommate, a short, mild, bookish boy named Howard. Like Sarah, Howard was Jewish. At that time, during the 1980s, Hyde Park was one of the most dangerous urban neighborhoods in the country. But Sarah and Howard didn't think much about what was happening around them. For one thing, Howard was earnestly liberal in his political attitudes. He was as hopeful about human nature as he was happy to be young. For another, both Howard and Sarah were devoted to their books. Their actual surroundings were remote to them. They were the ideal University of Chicago students. Their seriousness about Chicago's intellectual high-mindedness was what distinguished them from the other applicants who had written serious essays and obtained serious recommendations, yet who had failed to be admitted to the university's serious precincts.

Howard and Sarah were not romantically entangled. They studied twelve hours a day, and when they unwound, they relaxed by reading a classic novel. Their withdrawn temperaments gently bumped against each other like identical sealed containers. They needed someone who could pry the lid off their bookish absorption. They needed a cathartic opposite. Howard hadn't yet found that person. Sarah thought she had found him. His name was Karl.

Karl came from a working-class Polish American family. He was tall and supple-figured, conservative in his politics, ashamed of his family's anti-Semitism yet helplessly estranged from Jews. Having inherited an attitude that defined Sarah as unreachable, Karl found the prospect of intimacy with her irresistible. Karl spent most of his time at Sarah's apartment, where he and Howard ignored each other like two different species on separate biological tracks—they were like an emu sharing a barnyard with a mule.

Howard looked down on Karl's conservative politics. Since Karl never read serious books, Howard considered him a frivolous rube. He associated Karl's resentment of books and culture with Karl's wide-eyed discomfort around Jews. For his part, Karl scoffed at Howard's earnest liberalism. He especially

scorned Howard's seriousness. Karl, who was studying econom-
ics, wanted to be a banker. He retained a working-class disdain
for culture. He belonged, for instance, to a fraternity, and he and
his friends favored binge-drinking, fart jokes, and the occasional
gang bang. For Karl, the seriousness of books crumbled under
the transformative power of money. Aspiring to a better material life than his parents had, he found that money opened doors,
while culture stood in his way without promising anything concrete. Culture confused you by making you think at least twice
about everything.

Sarah's seriousness flattered Karl's vanity only to the extent
that he felt he owned it along with possessing Sarah. Owning it,
he could dismiss its importance. This proprietary feeling about
Sarah and her seriousness made Karl think that he was in love
with her. As for Sarah, Karl's lack of seriousness made her want
to care for him. It also reassured her that she could control him.

One broiling summer evening, when Karl was visiting, an intruder slipped through the window that Sarah and Howard had
bookishly left open. The intruder pulled out a gun and told Karl
and Howard to stand against the wall. He told Sarah to undress.
When she was naked, he tied her to a chair. He was sweating,
desperate, hopped up. Karl knew that if something didn't change
in the situation, Sarah would be raped and probably killed. He
waited a few seconds for something to change. When nothing
did, he realized in a surge of panic and adrenaline that he was the
only one who could make something happen. He lunged at the
intruder. The two of them began wrestling for the gun. Howard

joined them and the three of them whirled around the apartment, knocking over tables and lamps and stacks of books.

Suddenly Karl could feel Howard releasing his grasp. Howard fled out the front door. Karl continued to fight until the intruder broke away from him. The intruder ran back a few steps, stopped, and turned around. He aimed the gun point-blank at Karl and shot him. The bullet struck Karl in the neck. In the meantime, Sarah had untied herself and was screaming out the window. She was not screaming "Help!" or "Police!" Serious Sarah was just screaming, like an animal. The intruder pushed her aside and escaped out the window and down the fire escape.

Frivolous Karl lived and thrived. Sarah recovered and also thrived. The two of them went their separate ways. Serious Howard remains in serious therapy to this day.

Beatrice and Dante, Revisited

Beatrice married Dante when she was thirty-nine. Some of Dante's women friends quipped that he needed someone to pick up his shirts at the dry cleaner. In fact, Dante had finally gotten serious when he realized that he couldn't live without her. Dante had lived in New York long enough never to say something like "can't live without her" without adding several levels of irony to the phrase, but in this case, it was literally true. After a trip to Belize, he had been diagnosed with a rare, incurable disease.

Dante died about a year after he married Beatrice. She had gotten pregnant shortly after their marriage and gave birth to a boy a few months after Dante's death. From then on, she could not bear to hear the word "serious." For years she had waited for Dante to become serious about their relationship. Then she spent months hearing Dante's illness described as serious. When he was rushed to the hospital days before his death, the doctors told her, over and over, that Dante's condition was "serious."

Beatrice had then what used to be called an "epiphany," a moment of revelation that religious people believe is the result of an instant of grace. She realized that seriousness can only be a good in life when it is applied to human beings or to the products of human beings. When a situation becomes serious, it is always bad. This is because purposefulness is a human quality. When the impersonal becomes serious, it acquires a purpose—like illness, like catastrophic weather—and then purpose becomes monstrous.

From that moment on, Beatrice understood that humanity is in a constant struggle not only to live a serious life but also to protect itself against the monstrous seriousness of impersonal forces.

Seriousness in Pieces

Our public icons used to present standards of seriousness on which we modeled ourselves, or against which we rebelled. In a pinch, they could inspire or console someone like Beatrice. In the space of a single generation, however, our icons have gone from being simple, straightforward exemplars of a single quality to enigmas who exist in fragments, unknowable to us, perhaps even unknowable to themselves.

It used to be, not long ago, that we were content to allow our celebrated figures to serve as rudimentary moral guides to our national existence. Often, they simply stood for the proverbial

American promise of going somewhere from nowhere. By talking about them, we reassured ourselves about the possibilities of American life. Europe had the grandiose Age of Romanticism. We had the humbly born Marilyn, or Sinatra, or Elvis. We liked to crystallize an epoch in an individual as a way to offer individuals the hope of transcending their epoch.

Of course we knew there was more going on behind the scenes and under the surface. The gossip industry emitted steady inklings of Marilyn's bruising sex life, Sinatra's mob connections, Elvis's drug use and taste for prepubescent girls. But our own lives were so layered, nuanced, complex, and secretly startling that we let these sleeping dogs lie.

Back then, you might say that everyone, straight or gay, was, to one degree or another, in the closet where identity was concerned. We liked keeping public figures public; it certified our own sense of security about our private lives. Plus, we needed public myths, because they provided something simple to navigate by. They were a relief. Enjoying them made up a big part of our leisure time. If we wanted complexity, ambiguity, and nuance, we read a serious novel. An intuitive understanding of this public need to take our leaders seriously is perhaps why the Washington press corps turned a blind eye to JFK's chronic illness, and to his sexual dalliances in the White House.

Now the steady deluge of information has turned all our leisure time into work. We read the superficial revelations of chatter—or at least skim them—incessantly. The very volume of informational stuff makes it necessary to sift through it and determine what's true and what isn't. In the age of Sinatra, you read the paper or watched the evening news, reflected on what you read and watched, and then osmotically allowed it to settle into your picture of reality. That was what was known as leisure time. Now we read dozens of accounts of the same event as it's unfolding; we examine, analyze, compare. There's no time for leisure at all.

No time for judgment, either. Each version of an event gives way to another. Each interpretation of a person gives way to another. In the Cubist paintings of Picasso and Braque, stable portraits yielded to faces broken up into contrasting facial angles depicted simultaneously. Life itself has now become Cubistic. There are several Julian Assanges. Several Elizabeth Edwardses. Several Barack Obamas. One minute Mel Gibson is beating his girlfriend, and the next minute the gossip sites are sizzling with photos of him playing tenderly with his young daughter. Michael Jackson: Pathetic? Perverted? Princely? No wonder that when they release some new Nixon tapes every couple of years, commentators report on Nixon's racism and anti-Semitism with something like relief. His villainy is a kind of white Christmas. It is consistent, reliable, and predictable, just like the ones you used to know.

The cult of information now performs what used to be the serious novel's function. What with leaked e-mails, and Facebook pages, and memoirs, we see the public and private dimensions of people's lives simultaneously. You used to have to go to literary fiction for that.

Even as Elizabeth Edwards was trying publicly to weather the storm of her husband's betrayals with dignity, reporters Mark Halperin and John Heilemann were exposing selective episodes from her private life in their book *Game Change*. At one point, they depict her fighting with her husband in an airport and tearing open her blouse to show him her mastectomy scars, as she staggered, "nearly falling to the ground," in the two authors' words.

When Nixon's men had operatives break into the office of Daniel Ellsberg's psychiatrist, they were looking for the kind of information that has now become standard in mainstream journalism. A *New Yorker* profile of WikiLeaks founder Julian Assange came with all the detail necessary for a clinical diagnosis. Seeming to have never known his father, Assange was shaped by an unhealthy attachment to an unstable and nomadic mother, who combined her self-destructive impulses with an intolerance for any type of social or emotional relationship—except, maybe, the one with her son. Assange's subsequent antagonisms to his mother's second husband and her lovers sealed his fate as being helplessly driven against authority. Not long ago, it took decades to make public that kind of intimate material about someone. Can you imagine Daniel Ellsberg's mother telling a reporter, as Assange's mother told *The New Yorker*, that she was sure her son "has some PTSD that is untreated"?

We all thought we knew who John F. Kennedy was. Until history Cubistized him. Try to put your finger on Mr. Obama. Since he moved so many people with his seriousness during his presidential campaign, he has become Cubistized along with every other consequential public figure. He has been compared to, or compared himself to: JFK, FDR, Lincoln, Truman, Reagan, Carter, Clinton. He is (a) a socialist; (b) a capitalist tool;

(c) a soggy-eyed idealist; (d) a callous pragmatist; (e) a savior; (f) an arrogant elitist; (g) a downtrodden revolutionary; (h) a frantic amateur; (i) a cynical opportunist; (j) a determined avenger; (k) a cold-blooded murderer. A hero, and a villain.

It's unclear whether the new simultaneity of public and private adds up to anything truer than the old romantic opacity. But one thing is for sure. Just when you think you've put your finger on what makes one public figure or another serious, he or she breaks into a million contradictory meanings. The question is whether public figures like Obama have mastered the sincere performance of different roles or whether their refraction through the infinite venues of media, and through the countless layers of social and cultural expression, gives them the impression of malleability. It could be that our public figures seem to lack seriousness because we ourselves lack a stable means of seriously apprehending them.

CHAPTER FOUR
_____

The Three Pillars of Seriousness

As we have seen, the meaning of seriousness changes under the pressure of circumstance, character, and temperament. But through all the murkiness and gray zones of our lives, we seek it out. And through all the shifts and refractions and inflections of our quest to be serious and to be treated seriously, the essential elements of seriousness present themselves. They are: Attention, Purpose, and Continuity.

Test them. Take any situation or person that life presents you with and give it Siegel's Three Pillars of Seriousness Test. Try them out on the humble examples presented to you in this book. In Beatrice's desire that Dante get serious in their relationship, she is really asking for our three essentials.

Attention: She wants the project of building a family and therefore a future with Dante to be the only common enterprise he engages in with a woman. She wants him to regard her in the same full perspective in which she regards him. She wants them both to be three-dimensional to each other.

Purpose: She wants to feel that the fleeting moments of pleasure that she and Dante experience together are part of a larger flow of events. Pleasure promises everything and, in an instant, breaks every promise it makes. Beatrice wants to feel that her pleasurable moments have an undercurrent of permanence, a countermotion to mortality. Like everyone, she can wake up in the morning and make it through her day only by staking everything on the assumption that she will continue to live and that life will yield concrete improvements. Her essential relationships have to reflect that assumption.

Finally, continuity: She wants to be the same Beatrice every day. The persistence of her identity is the only way she can hope to affect the reality around her. Therefore, she wants her more crucial relationships with other people to reflect the sameness of her identity. She wants them to be, fundamentally, the same people day after day, which means that she requires them to exist in the same relation to her tomorrow as they do today.

Let us apply our three principles to Jackson, the romantically solitary painter who became a commercial artist and family man. You cannot make a work of art without immersing yourself in the process of creating it, without having a vision of what the completed object will be, without working at it day after day. Attention, purpose, continuity.

And you cannot marry and raise a family without immersing yourself in the process of creating one, without having a vision of what constitutes a happy, healthy child, without working at marriage and family day after day. As Simone Signoret tells Laurence Olivier in *Term of Trial*, "Love does not go on twenty-four hours a day." Oh, the French genius for romantic clarity. In other words, "love" does not exist. Rather, it consists of the sometimes-present, sometimes-absent experience—of the other person's kindness, or intelligence, or honesty, or reassuring presence, or wit, or physical chemistry—that keeps two people together. The only reality is fragile human life, meaningless except for the meanings we deluded and deluding people keep projecting onto it. We have to work at it. Attention, purpose, continuity. We have to be serious.

Karl's rescue of Sarah? Through all the clowning and frivolity of his frat-boy existence, through all the superficiality of his pursuit of money, Karl attained a seriousness of being that gave the lie to the intellectual's exclusive claim on seriousness. The sudden fixity of his mind grasped every detail of the unfolding situation just as an artistic genius will envision, in a flash, every overlapping and interlocking detail of the work of art he is laboring to bring into being. Karl's purpose was to save Sarah's life. He began the quick work of saving her and followed through to the unforeseen end. Howard, the intellectual, didn't.

The dignified incongruity of Sidney Morgenbesser's joke to the policeman was also the result of our Three Pillars. The philosopher's entire being was focused on the seriousness of the problem that lay before him. His purpose was to commune with the policeman over a profound idea. His capacity for weaving a joke out of intellectual history into the present moment created a shared continuity that was larger than both he and the officer.

You can apply the same criteria in the same way to the cop's enforcement of the law.

My boyhood confrontation with the street gang provides a counterexample. My persecutor did not live up to the Three Pillars. His attention was on the mark all right, but his sense of purpose did not extend beyond the brief moment of hurting me. And his deed had no use for continuity. Acts of destruction, even the sustained, purposeful act of genocide, traduce the future; they violate the principle of continuity. That is why there is no such thing as seriousness in an activity that is destructive to anyone or anything that lives. A "serious" crime is really a contradiction in terms.

My bookishness on that day proved to be my momentary downfall. But the cultivation of my intellect and imagination that was advanced by reading useless Tolstoy got me up and out into the world. Seriousness can be a quiet and humble achievement. The disconnect between seriousness and status is one of the reasons why seriousness is so elusive, as people pursue the latter in the mistaken belief that by doing so, they will attain the former.

We say we want meaning in our lives. Some of us seek it through religious faith, others through secular projects. But what both the religious and the secular quest have in common is the search for seriousness. And the three essences of that search are Attention, Purpose, and Continuity, through any circumstance, and in any situation.

A Word About Silly

Silly is not the opposite of serious. Laughter is the opposite of serious. Silly is something different: it is the enemy of serious. That makes silly the enemy of laughter. The hint of mischief Beerbohm put on Matthew Arnold's face stopped at the border of silliness.

Silliness—the silliness of the Three Stooges—makes us shake our heads. Antic mischief—the antic mischief of the Marx Brothers, or of Buster Keaton, or of Laurel and Hardy—makes us laugh. If you think Harpo's muteness, a condition that is often the result of deep mental trauma, is not a streak of dark seriousness amid all the humor, then you are giving silly too much credit.

You are talking with someone and you want to see whether he is serious. So you start to look for the purpose in his speech and actions; you begin wondering what his motives are. You try to figure out what the consequences of his conduct will be. You pay attention to his every word, and you start thinking about his context: Who is he? What was he in the past? What does he want to be in the future? What will he be in the future? Your expectation is that whatever he does will be shot through with rationality. It will make sense. You will be able to understand it.

Such seriousness does not mean that whatever relationship you enter into with this person—in the realms of friendship, love, business, law, et cetera—will be solemn. The element of play will gradually become part of your bond of seriousness. In his classic 1938 book *Homo Ludens* ("Man the Playing Animal"), the Dutch historian Johan Huizinga observes that nearly all human activity partakes of play. Even children's games, wrote Huizinga, are played "in profound seriousness." This is because, Huizinga believed, "play is a voluntary activity which takes place within certain fixed limits of time and space [and] has nothing to do with necessity, utility or duty."

Genuine seriousness is also free from the pressures of necessity, utility, or duty. You are not serious when you are plunging a backed-up toilet. You are just doing what you have to do because you need the usefulness of a toilet. But there is no concrete necessity to be serious about anything. You choose to be serious the way you choose to keep living. Play and seriousness are both types of freedom; play is the intuitive and improvisatory side of seriousness. You can only understand your serious individual if you play with her or him, as it were—in business, in friendship, in love—and explore all the avenues and angles of the situation you are building together.

Without the element of authentic play, authentic seriousness does not exist. As we shall see in a moment, seriousness without play is silly.

Laughter, not play, is the real opposite of seriousness. You might say that laughter is negative seriousness. Seriousness asserts the true, sincere, and authentic, while laughter obliterates the false, insincere, and inauthentic. Matthew Arnold himself, early in his career, before he spoke only of "high seriousness," wrote of "cheerful seriousness." In *Ulysses*, James Joyce coined the term "jocoseriousness." In his satirical cartoon of Arnold, Beerbohm sought to remind the moralist of his earlier emphasis on wit.

Laughter and seriousness, two opposites, need each other like day and night, autumn and spring; they need each other the way man and woman do for the purpose of procreation. As Plato put it, "I say that about serious matters a man should be serious, and about a matter which is not serious, he should not be serious." That's not a knee-slapper, but you know what he means. Laughter and seriousness each has its necessary place in relation to the other.

Silliness is at its most silly not when it provokes laughter, but when it is the performance of seriousness. I would say that this ultimate silliness is seriousness in drag, but that would make it too close to "camp." Even camp, that mostly gay style popular in the sixties and seventies, was, at bottom, serious. Camp flaunted artifice, irony, theatricality, for the purpose of . . . undermining seriousness. Which was a very serious project. The only intellectual to have thought explicitly about how to be serious in modern American life, Susan Sontag, once wrote that "the whole point of Camp is to dethrone the serious. Camp is playful, anti-serious." Fine. Anti-serious. But then she went on to say that "more precisely, Camp involves a new, more complex relation to 'the serious.' . . . One can be serious about the frivolous, frivolous about the serious." That is a sentiment the most conservative cleric in the most orthodox branch of any of the world's major religions would not take exception to. A more complex relation to the serious! How wonderfully, marvelously, admirably serious!

No, today's silly is not camp, and it is not *The Three Stooges*, either. Rather, it is the earnest performance of seriousness in the absence of both genuine seriousness and real laughter. I'm thinking of people who defy Plato's advice to not be serious about unserious matters and feel that, to win approval, they have to appear serious all the time. Often this facade of seriousness is in direct proportion to their utter frivolity. Think Keith Olbermann. Think Glenn Beck. Think, in a different key entirely, Oprah. The grave, urgent seriousness of all three is in direct proportion to each one's special brand of theatrics.

Contrast this with the appearance of frivolousness in direct proportion to an utter seriousness. When the poet Allen Ginsberg, who was gay, wrote at the end of one of his poems, "America I'm putting my queer shoulder to the wheel," he was puncturing the stuffy gravitas of that old saying, "Put your shoulder to the wheel," and transferring its core of seriousness to people who were previously excluded from it. He was mocking stale seriousness for the sake of introducing a fresh, new seriousness. Ginsberg may have often liked to play the clown, but he was rarely silly.

Silliness, on the other hand, is the giggle that you faintly detect behind the gravitas.

You cannot help but feel this giggle behind the gravitas of novelists who write "literary" novels in which a convoluted density of language is a parody of The Literary. Behind the *seriousness* of politicians who substitute words for actions and then make fools of themselves on the late-night comedy shows. Behind the *seriousness* of intellectuals who pour all their conceptual energy into appearing serious and then run with the most influential herd. Behind the *seriousness* of television pundits who impersonate seriousness in the form of extremist ranting—and the fawning print journalists who serve as their foils. Behind the *seriousness* of the constant exposure of public figures' private foibles.

From every corner of society, silliness prances back and forth as the empty form of a seriousness that has been exhausted, worn out. "Silliness" traces its origins back to a Middle English word meaning "happy, blessed, innocent, pitiable, feeble." Underneath the inanity, the unmeaning of our American silliness, is an implacable desire to win approval and even love by appearing vulnerably and guilelessly wedded to the highest ideals of seriousness.

Look at it this way. Mozart was one of the most serious human beings who ever lived, and he was also one of the silliest. During performances of *The Magic Flute*, he stood in the wings, making loud farting noises with his mouth to try and get the singers to collapse in laughter. Mozart knew exactly where silliness belonged in relation to seriousness. In the wings. Now imagine a different situation. Imagine Mozart's audiences settling themselves in their seats at the theater to find, when the curtain went up, Mozart himself standing on the stage making loud farting noises, while the singers linger quietly offstage. He is doing this with, as Matthew Arnold would say, absolute sincerity and in an attitude of total seriousness. The orchestra is also accompanying him in absolute sincerity and with total seriousness. The entire atmosphere is one of the highest high seriousness.

That is our Age of Silly. In our desperation to be serious and to find seriousness, we uneasily settle for its impersonation. Which makes us long for seriousness with greater intensity, at the same time that we mistrust its sincerity all the more when we think we might have found it.

CHAPTER FIVE

A Brief, Eccentric History of Seriousness

Every age and every culture has its forms of public seriousness. They shape the individual's sense of what it means to be serious. But for centuries, no one thought to exhort people to be serious, or to try to define what seriousness was.

Plato uses the ancient Greek equivalent of "serious" and "seriousness" nine times in *The Republic*. Aristotle uses them thirteen times in the *Nicomachean Ethics* and four times in the *Poetics*. The two words occur four times in John Stuart Mill's *On Liberty*, and five times in David Hume's *An Enquiry Concerning the Principles of Morals*. Their German counterparts appear twice in Kant's *Critique of Pure Reason*. In the King James Version of the Bible, you find only the word "serious," which occurs seven times.

That includes the Old and the New Testaments. Neither word is used at all in the Constitution of the United States, the Declaration of Independence, or the Bill of Rights.

It seems that the more elusive seriousness is, the more frequently it is invoked. It never occurred to Plato or the authors of the Bible that seriousness was a special state of being, let alone that it was an elusive and ambiguous one. On the other hand, Allan Bloom's 1987 sensational bestseller, *The Closing of the American Mind*, is a lament over the disappearance of seriousness from American culture in which the words "serious" and "seriousness" appear eighty-one times.

Despite the Greek philosophers' reticence on the subject, we have an idea of what it meant to be serious in ancient Greece. Plato's figure of the "philosopher-king" and Aristotle's "great-souled man" are both models of reasonableness and moderation. The Greeks held the individual who restrained his passions in high regard. Their tragic heroes always meet their doom on account of bad tempers: furious Achilles, impulsive King Oedipus, vindictive Clytemnestra.

It's no coincidence that in his celebrated funeral speech, Pericles, the Athenian statesman and general, uses the word "anger" again and again. "I expected this outbreak of anger against me," he tells the Athenians, who have grown disenchanted with him. In his subtle way, Pericles is telling them that they are not in the right frame of mind to be serious. He himself is, however. He contrasts their anger with his ability to reason. "So far as I am concerned, if you are angry with me, you are angry with one who has, I think, at least as much ability as anyone to see what ought to be done, and to explain what he sees." To do and to explain. To act and to think while you are acting. That is another Greek ideal of seriousness.

The Greeks are often presented as paragons of seriousness who exalted the power of the mind. That is not exactly right. Socrates, Athens's gadfly philosopher, made it his job to puncture such official seriousness, all in the name of being serious.

Anytime Socrates encountered someone who spoke with confidence about a certain idea, he would question that person mercilessly until their seriousness was exposed as confusion or self-delusion. He used irony to flush out illogic. These encounters were collected by Plato, Socrates' student, who wrote them up into dialogues. At the end of each dialogue, the conventionally serious understanding of a concept such as "love," or "truth," or "beauty" has been so challenged by Socrates that the target of his inquisition doesn't know whether he is coming or going. Socrates agreed with other Greeks that seriousness was identical to reason, but with one difference. For Socrates' countrymen, reason meant certainty. For Socrates, it meant doubt. One thing led to another, and Socrates' interrogations began to make the officially serious men of Athens look foolish, vain, and not serious at all.

Inevitably, Socrates was brought to trial on trumped-up charges of corrupting the youth of his day and of holding irreverent attitudes toward religion. After hearing Socrates' spirited defense of himself, the Athenian court sentenced him to death by drinking hemlock. Socrates' friends offered him an opportunity to flee to safety, but he refused. It was time to die, he said. He had lived out his span of life. And, he added, since the purpose of philosophy is to reconcile man to his mortality, what kind of serious philosopher fears death? Finally, he explained that since he had agreed to live under Athens's laws, he had an obligation to die under them.

Socrates represents the two faces of Western seriousness. He identifies seriousness with reasoning power and moral courage. And he associates it with an ironic deflation of what passes for public seriousness.

For centuries after the death of Socrates, the image of seriousness in the West proceeded, in varying degrees, along those two contrapuntal lines. There was the sanctified, public form of seriousness that had started out fresh with rationality and moral force, and then hardened into the official picture of reality. This was usually exemplified by statesmen, generals, various degrees of royalty, and religious figures. There was always a certified class of thinkers, too, who reflected this conventional wisdom. They embodied the official seriousness. In Socrates' time, they were known as the Sophists. And then there was the unofficial serious, but no less public, puncturing of the former. The puncturing was usually done by philosophers, literati, and entertainers, and later by religious iconoclasts.

Like the old *Mad* magazine series "Spy vs. Spy," one type of seriousness has always been at war with the other. As Roman emperors celebrated the virtues of wisdom and valor, Roman satirists like Horace, Juvenal, and Petronius exposed the corruption and self-interest of "wise" public men. The moral seriousness of Christ overthrew the moral seriousness of the Pharisees. In the conflict between Galileo and the Catholic Church, the rational seriousness of science did battle with the ethical gravity of religion.

In every case, the measure of seriousness was the degree to which each party maintained a high level of attention, purpose, and continuity. As the Roman Empire degenerated into moral chaos, attention gave way to distraction, purpose to confusion, continuity to fragmented moments of physical gratification. The rebellious Jews who followed Christ resented the way the Pharisees had withdrawn their attention, redirected their purpose, and severed their sense of continuity from the interests of the poor. The medieval church had allowed attention to become ignorance, purpose to turn into fanaticism, and continuity to be applied only to the institution of the church itself.

In revolt against the church's ignorance and fanaticism, the Enlightenment culminated in the emotional ignorance and hyperrational fanaticism of the French Revolution. In response, the Romantics came along and made feeling, not reason, the touchstone of truth. The pendulum had swung again. Descartes' Enlightenment war cry, "I think, therefore I am," gave way to Rousseau's reply, "I feel my heart, therefore I understand humankind." Of course, the proclamation of either principle in the wrong age would elicit the incredulous or sardonic reply, "Are you serious?"

With the advent of the Romantic era came another phase in the unfolding of Western seriousness. Now the artist, once regarded with suspicion along with pimps and thieves, became an officially serious person himself. When the English Romantic poet Percy Bysshe Shelley declared that poets were the "unacknowledged legislators of mankind," he was being modest. Lord

Byron had the status of a rock star. Napoleon came to pay his respects to Goethe after conquering Prussia. Émile Zola's polemics shook French politics and society. But having attained the status of official seriousness, the artist was now in danger of turning into a caricature of seriousness himself.

Science finally began to conquer religion in the nineteenth century. Then came the First World War. The war's murderous technology, and the hypocritical intellectual arguments that had led to war, destroyed faith in science and rationality. Now seriousness was defined by anything that outraged what passed for seriousness. Satisfying the desire for sex and violence was elevated over self-restraint. The workings of the unconscious were celebrated over logic and reason. Disgusted exposure of what was believed to be a universal human urge to murder and steal was valued above arguments for the nobility of man. One type of seriousness replaced another.

It could be that seriousness is vulnerable to physical laws, like bread. It grows stale when left out too long. Almost five hundred years ago, the Dutch philosopher Erasmus, in his "In Praise of Folly," lamented instances in which one could "go to church and hear sermons, in which if there be anything serious delivered, the audience is either asleep, yawning, or weary of it; but if the preacher—pardon me, I almost said declaimer—as too often happens, fall but into an old wives' tale, they're presently awake, prick up their ears and gape after it." Yet he went on to complain, with wry irony, about the type of "poetical saint" who is "more religiously worshiped than Peter, Paul, or even Christ himself." In other words, the perennial freshness of even tall tales trumps a seriousness that has hardened into pious platitudes.

Along with the waxing and waning elements of seriousness, there was another constant in the war between the two seriousnesses. The rebellion against a seriousness that had become official and had lost its vitality often came from ordinary people. It originated with people cut off from the inner sanctums of privilege and connection. The seriousness they were rebelling against was the province of elites. After a time, the rebels themselves formed an elite class. Then the dynamic began again. A different group of ordinary people rebelled. And the new elites fell to the wave of new seriousness.

Many of the Jews who followed Christ protested the elitist Pharisees. These Jews, in turn, eventually became the Christians who turned the Catholic Church into the mightiest hierarchy the world had ever known. The itinerant Enlightenment intellectuals who fomented the French Revolution turned into elites who sentenced tens of thousands to death in order to consolidate their power in a new order. The middle-class Romantics, some of whom completed the French Revolution in the 1840s, swept Europe clean of the aristocratic elite and became the oppressive industrialist elite of Dickens's novels, who paid lip service throughout the nineteenth century to humanist ideals of truth, beauty, and justice. The Modernists who tore apart humanism's hollow precepts after the First World War became the literary, artistic, and intellectual elites of the postwar period. Their descendants are the cultural elites of today.

You might even say that once a certain form of seriousness becomes an institutionalized style of seriousness, it is, by definition, just this side of silly.

Seriousness American-style

Up until now, we have been talking about European forms of seriousness. In America, seriousness is a whole different story. This is because the search for freedom, rather than the quest for stability, is at the center of American life.

In Europe, the objective was always to establish some kind of order: from the Roman Empire to the Catholic Church to the mercantile system of the Renaissance to the nation-states of today. People came to America to escape, literally, what historians came to call the "old order" of class privilege. The Pilgrims came here to find religious freedom. The American colonists rebelled to win political freedom. Waves of immigrants fled to American shores to find freedom in all of its dimensions. From the counterculture demonstrations of the 1960s to the Tea Party protests of today, the American goal has always been to expand the limits of the individual's arena of action.

American civilization is, by definition, a work in progress. A daily dynamic of creative chaos runs through it. European civilization is, by definition, a bulwark against chaos. In France, for example, civilization is so invincible, so eternal, that this immutable stability makes opposition to it all the more cheerfully ferocious. You can hurl the most incredible rhetorical and intellectual violence against French custom and convention and still have time for some conversation in the café, *un peu de vin*, a delicious dinner, and, of course, *l'amour*. And in the morning, you extricate yourself from such sophisticated coddling—the result of centuries of art and artifice—and rush back to the theoretical barricades. Civilization will always be there, having created its own domesticated forms of chaos. The refinement of pleasure plays a special role. Cooking and lovemaking as arts, for example, appease people by giving them the illusion of controlling their fate through the gratification of their senses. In Europe, to live seriously is to create public order through the private regimentation of the spirit. The Marquis de Sade routinized carnality.

American civilization is a new wrinkle in the history of seriousness. On the one hand, the practical individual is considered the most serious individual. Freedom is thought to be won only through the ambitious mastery of the facts. From J. P. Morgan to Bill Gates, the titans of industry are serious. The financiers and businessmen are serious. These sometimes ruthless figures, driven by gigantic appetites, know how to control and channel the appetites of their fellow men into commerce. Far from seeking stability, they pursue constant forward-motion through perpetual innovation. They make their own freedom, and by doing so, enlarge everyone else's.

And there is the rub in American seriousness.

Our emphasis on practical life makes us fear the effects of crude materialism. We become afraid that we do not have the high aspirations of the old civilizations from whence we came. Does our life come down to one transaction after another, we ask ourselves? As a result, we put an almost fanatical value on the importance of culture. From the Great Books curriculum invented by Robert Maynard Hutchins at the University of Chicago, to the Harvard Classics, to Allan Bloom's *The Closing of the American Mind*, to Harold Bloom's *The Western Canon*, we associate the classic literature of Western civilization with nothing less than moral renewal and spiritual salvation. In our fear that we care only for practical matters, we make culture a practical matter of self-improvement.

Such ambivalence is rooted in our Puritan forebears. Their Calvinism made them insist on spiritual introspection—culture, if you will—yet also caused them to consider worldly success the mark of spiritual triumph. Lack of wealth indicated idleness. Idleness was Satan's field of operations.

This mistrust of idleness gave birth to the Protestant work ethic that was the dominant form of public seriousness in America for nearly two hundred years, exemplified by religious figures and statesmen. These days, we like to think of George Washington and Abraham Lincoln as two distinct forms of American seriousness. Washington is the practical man, quick to action; Lincoln is the reflective man, anguishing, under the aspect of eternity, over what might be the moral course of action. But in all probability, the contemporaries of both figures saw the same social type: the man of humble origins rising through the world by dint of hard work and shrewd, rapid judgment. After all, our perception of Lincoln as brooding, tortured, and ambivalent is based on the gradual exfoliation of his private life through many decades of scholarship. Perhaps we like that version of Lincoln because it is a compliment we pay to our own self-image as serious people indifferent to practical matters. But Lincoln, a Republican who was a bootstraps individualist, was supremely practical. Even his eloquence, the metaphysical power of which nearly stuns us, echoes with the standard—and politically effective—biblical cadences of his day.

Then there was the other American seriousness, the anti-serious seriousness of, say, Mark Twain. His *Adventures of Huckleberry Finn* was a dark, macabrely humorous evisceration of the official seriousness of his day. It dismantled the staled seriousness of the cleric, the statesman, the businessman. This other American seriousness sought out, with desperate passion, modes of creative idleness or anarchy outside the pale of practicality.

Allen Ginsberg expressed the search for that Archimedean point of seriousness with wry playfulness:

> *Are you going to let our emotional life be run by Time*
> *Magazine?*
> *I'm obsessed by Time Magazine.*
> *I read it every week.*
> *Its cover stares at me every time I slink past the corner*
> *candystore.*
> *I read it in the basement of the Berkeley Public Library.*
> *It's always telling me about responsibility. Businessmen are*
> *serious.*
> *Movie producers are serious. Everybody's serious but me.*

Against American practical seriousness, with its roots in Puritan worldliness and the Protestant work ethic, Ginsberg conjured a different kind of seriousness. He had in mind a conscientiousness about the purpose of one's life and its relationship to the world around it. This would be the seriousness of *ser*, a clarity of purpose about the why and the how of being in the world, expressed through the qualities of attention, purpose, and continuity. It is what we have called organic seriousness. To be sure, there was a practical dimension to Ginsberg's quest for spiritual self-improvement, too. To some extent, he was Horatio Alger in beads.

As older civilizations matured, intellectuals acquired the respectability of a separate class unto themselves. The religious scholar or cleric metamorphosed into the secular thinker. The first intellectuals were men of the Enlightenment who rebelled against the seriousness of church. They were individuals who, literally, thought for a living, thanks to the largesse of wealthy patrons.

Which brings us to yet another unique quality of American seriousness. By the twentieth century, Europeans could look to several social types as paragons of seriousness: statesmen, military figures, religious figures, artists, and intellectuals. In America, it was not until after the Second World War that the life of the mind came into its own as an exemplary serious activity.

There were two reasons for the rise of the American intellectual as a serious figure in the postwar period: the GI Bill and the Cold War. The GI Bill made higher education possible for millions of American soldiers who, because of financial limitations, might never have been able to attend college. It fostered a universal hunger to be educated and created an avid audience for serious writing and thinking. The horror of war had instilled in these veterans—and in many other Americans, too—a yearning to acquire knowledge for its own sake. The senselessness of suffering and violent death made intimate the problems of truth, beauty, good, and evil, of the meaning and purpose of life. Such questions became more urgent than making a buck. This was especially true since making a buck amid the unprecedented prosperity after the war was easier than it had ever been for so many people.

The Cold War had an opposite yet complementary effect to the GI Bill. Rather than making thinking an alternative to business, it invested thinking with the urgency of business. Rivalry between the United States and the Soviet Union was not just an obscure geopolitical conflict, best left to politicians and their advisers. It was an emergency that every citizen had to be vigilant about understanding.

To comprehend the antagonism between America and the Soviet Union, you had to do more than read the newspaper or watch the evening news on the new medium known as television. You had to understand the antagonism between capitalism and communism. That is to say, you had to know something about European history and ideas. You had to know something about the character of American freedom. The Cold War elevated intellectual debate from an activity engaged in by high school nerds with no aptitude for varsity sports to a vital, even glamorous—it was said that JFK read the French novelist André Malraux while putting on his tie in the morning!—matter of state.

With the expansion of higher education and the intellectual rigors of the Cold War came the shaping of middle-class taste. Even as serious intellectuals lamented the ascendancy of what they called "mass culture"—radio, TV, movies, glossy magazines, comic books, jazz—other intellectuals were using mass media to make seriousness available to nonintellectuals. It was the age of the University of Chicago Great Books, Will and Ariel Durant's *The*

Story of Civilization, *Reader's Digest*, Clifton Fadiman's *Lifetime Reading Plan*. Yet all these exercises in accessible knowledge also had the characteristic American purpose of self-improvement. As Americans were heeding President Kennedy's exhortations to stay physically fit in competition with the Russians, they were developing their minds and taste for the same purpose.

They were also competing with Europe in general just as much as with the Russians. Having rescued a Europe in ruins, Americans were no longer impressed by the edifice of European seriousness. The Cold War created divisions in American politics and culture that still persist, but its singular virtue was to turn a parochial country into a cosmopolitan one.

For some people today, this postwar period was a Golden Age of American Seriousness. The means of reflection were made available to all. Everyone could step outside the routine of buying and selling into a clear space where they could figure out who they were, and where they stood in the scheme of things.

But America is no less vulnerable to the cycles of seriousness and serious anti-seriousness than were older civilizations. As the First World War had done earlier, the Vietnam War, and the hypocrisy and lies surrounding it, engendered what became known as a "counterculture." As with European Modernism, the counterculture celebrated everything that ran counter to middle-class mores: sexual promiscuity, violence, irrationality, an "anti-art" that prided itself not on comforting Great Books gravitas but on anger, provocation, and outrage.

Some people located the end of American seriousness in the countercultural sixties. Others saw the counterculture as a new wave of seriousness, which they called "commitment." In their eyes, the creations of middle-class taste excluded broad swaths of American society, such as blacks, women, gays. The adherents of the new counterculture did not believe that culture could be serious if society was unjust. For them, commitment—i.e., self-less political engagement—was seriousness in action. Still others believed that without the universal enlightenment of middle-class taste, the countercultural revolution would never have begun in the first place. They believed that social justice always lags behind artistic and intellectual seriousness. Which is what makes the latter all the more precious.

In the late eighties and nineties, the rift opened by the social upheaval of the sixties played itself out in institutionalized form. The radicals who associated seriousness with commitment became tenured professors fighting for equal representation of minorities in both the student population and the curriculum. And the middle class that had been stunned into silence by the counterculture's theatrics found advocates in culturally conservative intellectuals who were well funded by powerful conservative foundations. It was one type of institutionalized, encrusted seriousness against another.

But the word "seriousness" had become anathema to the academic Left. They associated it with the white, male, Christian high seriousness of Matthew Arnold. They had no use, either, for Beerbohm's playful improvisation on Arnold. For them, "seriousness" was a mask for abusive power.

It was the cultural conservatives who took up the word "serious" and made it their battle cry. In fact, they associated it with the white, male, Christian high seriousness of Matthew Arnold. They had no use, either, for Beerbohm's playful improvisation on Arnold. For them, "seriousness" meant high culture, and high culture was the essential quality of beneficent authority.

This, however, was not the positive middlebrow seriousness of Robert Maynard Hutchins and his Great Books. Rather, it was the dour seriousness of a defensive posture. For the cultural conservatives, the preservation of high culture did not mean the elevation of leisure time. It meant nothing less than the preservation of American civilization. There was a police aspect to this incarnation of seriousness. Just as crumbling American cities in the seventies had needed more policemen on the streets, the cultural conservatives believed that crumbling American mores needed more policemen in the universities.

Because the academic Left abhorred the word "serious," they inadvertently kept it safe from travesty and traducement. But the advent of the cultural conservatives' emergency seriousness spelled the death of seriousness as a public style. The cultural conservatives didn't regard seriousness as organic, as a form of absolute attention in any positive realm of action, or even as a sudden access of grace. They thought of seriousness as having a separate existence itself, like a real thing—like some appliance called Serious, or an ointment. To be serious, you had to start out Serious. Seriousness was no longer a natural quality of existence that occurred along an infinite spectrum of experiences. It was a social and cultural imperative that dispensed morality as though it were an antibacterial soap.

The problem was that a great deal would have to be left out of, say, a college curriculum that dispensed moral seriousness. For one thing, you couldn't have the pagan poet-philosopher Lucretius and the Christian poet Milton on the same list. Too confusing. Nor could you have Plato's *Symposium*, where drunkenness, homosexual love, and sexual promiscuity are celebrated, and where the reigning comedian of Socrates' day, the comic playwright Aristophanes, has many of the best lines. Dante, who has a devil in hell make a "trumpet of his ass," would certainly have to go. And Shakespeare. And Rabelais. And Baudelaire. And D. H. Lawrence. And Kafka. Stop me before I get too serious about all the serious literature that uses laughter and tears to rip seriousness to shreds.

The pendulum of seriousness being what it is, an entire culture of dissent rose up against this neoconservative seriousness. It exalted ellipsis, indirection, and, above all, irony. The premise of this anti-seriousness was that any type of serious statement hid several levels of meaning that had the effect of canceling out the serious import. So the new anti-seriousness deployed irony to hint at unseen dimensions of seriousness. You weren't serious unless you were using irony to make the point that the appearance of seriousness was the telltale sign of being unserious.

The new serious-ironic anti-seriousness never gathered itself up into a permanent public form of seriousness. If you were being ironic and not saying what you meant, then no one could trust what anyone else was saying. People became alarmed. Symposia were organized, conferences convened, books written, experts consulted. Finally, the attacks on September 11 inspired some people, despite their horror, to breathe a sigh of relief that irony had been vanquished, and that a new era of seriousness was being ushered in.

But having been discredited by the conservatives once, and then discredited a second time by the ironists, seriousness once again had trouble getting off the ground as a new public style. For many people, 9/11 created an atmosphere in which seriousness was really just a mask for military opportunism and political expediency. Others despaired of any type of seriousness that did not bear the ultimately distracting onus of political analysis. The attempt to re-serious the culture fell flat on its face. For perhaps the first time in the history of Western civilization—I told you this was an eccentric account of seriousness—the vigorous unfolding of seriousness and serious anti-seriousness came to a halt. We were left with an entirely new movement that you might call "Whateverism." What would Socrates, the formidable interrogator, have done with that response?

Now there is an idea. To paraphrase a serious poet, perhaps our beginning is in our end. Perhaps, at this static point in time, a mental experiment is in order. What if we went back to Socrates himself and posed the question: "Are you serious?"

If you remember, Socrates explained to his friends that he had chosen to drink the hemlock and kill himself rather than flee to safety because, since he had lived under Athenian law, he was obligated to die under it. Here is where I would address our question. Was Socrates serious about killing himself to affirm the justice of Athenian law? I like to imagine that he was more serious than that. By declaring that he was killing himself in accordance with the law, he was demonstrating that any law that would order a true philosopher to destroy himself was inhuman and unjust. His final act fused irony and logic in the face of a monstrous seriousness.

In one stroke, Socrates had made ironic anti-serious seriousness the most serious gesture of all. And he did so in the spirit of, as Matthew Arnold put it, "absolute sincerity." He gave his life out of love for the truth. Or, to put it less exaltedly, he proved that seriousness was not some abstract style, or mood, or tone. It was a way of living. Socrates fulfilled his destiny in his work.

Let's think about that as we proceed.

CHAPTER SIX

Seriousness in Culture

I hope that by now I've handled the words "serious" and "seriousness" carefully enough to win your trust that I can talk about them seriously without becoming merely silly. It's not easy. The default mode of the most advanced critical writing nowadays is something like a triple self-consciousness. If you have anything serious to say, you have to begin by cutely distancing yourself from the type of people who say what you are about to say. Then you say it.

Everyone is so-over-it and three-steps-ahead-of-it. This is because, as Susan Sontag put it nearly fifty years ago, we have become "culturally oversaturated." She meant that every experience, idea, and social type has been represented in movies, or books, or journalism. You cannot talk about fundamental experiences without first asserting that you are aware of all the ways in which they have been represented, banalized, and trivialized. Consider the word "serious" itself. If you want to say that someone is known for being serious, but really isn't, you would hold up two fingers of each hand and wiggle them in the air as you call him a "serious" man. Yet you would also have to make the same gesture if you wanted sincerely to say that he is indeed a serious man. In that case, you would put quotation marks around "serious," to show that you know how it has been used, overused, and abused but that, despite the word's sullied history, you can confidently say that here is someone truly serious.

Quotation marks deployed in this way are perhaps the worst enemy of contemporary seriousness. (I helplessly use them all the time.) No wonder another name for qualifying quotation marks is "scare quotes." They scare you away from speaking sincerely about anything.

In the precincts of advanced taste—I mean, "advanced taste"—I cannot, for example, sincerely write about someone's avowed commitment to another person, or to a relationship. I have to write about someone's avowed "commitment." The quotation marks acknowledge that I know, from countless Hollywood romantic comedies, and from countless knowing magazine articles, that declarations of commitment are not worth the paper they are never written on. The scare quotes mean that I am aware of all the cultural representations of commitment that have deconstructed its real meaning. I am saying, Yes, I have seen Jennifer Aniston's annual romantic comedies, and *30 Rock*, and *The Departed*; I have seen all of these cultural representations' comical and tragic explorations of broken loyalties—but somewhere, buried in countless folds of reality, is real commitment. It would be even more effective for me to say (redundantly enough) that someone is seriously committed, that they are committed in the original, fresh, uncorrupted, unrepresented meaning of commitment. Unless of course they are only *known* for being remarkably committed, and are not really committed at all. Then I would say that they are "seriously" committed.

Even culture figures themselves, no matter how accomplished they are, see their reputations accrue quotation marks if they live long enough, the way hair will start to grow out of your ears if you live long enough. As we shall see, John Updike lived to see himself become "John Updike." His artistic worth became questioned simply because he had, you might say, been publicly over-represented. His seriousness staled into "seriousness."

Indeed, of all the familiar terms with which we are surrounded, the word "serious" is among the most idealized and the most abused. As a result, it almost has scare quotes sewn onto it.

There was a time when you could use the word "serious" without blinking an eye. After the Second World War, with the rise of the GI Bill and the growth of middlebrow culture, intellectuals acquired the respectability of seriousness that politicians also possessed. Intellectual journals like *Partisan Review* and *Commentary*, literary and social critics like Lionel and Diana Trilling, Norman Podhoretz, and Alfred Kazin became the respected exemplars of seriousness. Esoteric artistic movements like Abstract Expressionism spilled out into *Life* magazine and, though often derided, lodged themselves in the popular consciousness as styles of serious expression. Refined intellectuals like Dwight Macdonald and Harold Rosenberg wrote frequently for the middlebrow *New Yorker* magazine, which, in turn, published challenging, socially and politically consequential essays on poverty and the environment. Serious intellectuals like Kazin and Irving Howe might have deplored the popular assimilation of Abstract Expressionists such as Jackson Pollock and the commercial success of *The Catcher in the Rye* and similar serious novels. (Which success made critics like Kazin and Howe instinctively doubt such books' seriousness.) But the universal embrace of high artistic and intellectual style reflected a universal sincerity about wanting to live and think seriously.

Several developments put scare quotes around that innocent perception of seriousness. One was the movement of the visual arts toward a pure formalism, away from even the emotional content of the Abstract Expressionists. Almost thirty years ago, an event occurred in New York that brought the tension between popular and high art to the breaking point. That was when the federal government commissioned the highly regarded sculptor Richard Serra to build a work of art for New York City's Federal Plaza. The ensuing controversy marked an utter transformation of the meaning of seriousness in the arts.

Serra came up with *Tilted Arc*, a curving wall of naked steel 120 feet long and 12 feet high, which he placed in the middle of the vast urban space. The people who worked in the offices around the plaza, and who relaxed there during lunch and coffee breaks, protested. They said that Serra's work broke up the small vista that soothed their burdened minds and nerves. They called for the government to remove it. Serra himself agreed that *Tilted Arc* did not have a calming effect. "The viewer," he said, "becomes aware of himself and of his movement through the plaza. . . . Step by step the perception not only of the sculpture but of the entire environment changes." Art unsettles, disorients, and reorients.

Serra arrogantly refused to budge. Eight years and a sprawling controversy later, a panel convened by the U.S. General Services Administration, which had commissioned the sculpture, ruled that it should be taken down. An angry Serra declared: "I don't think it is the function of art to be pleasing." Serra was, and is, a very serious artist. Yet there was no bridge between his seriousness and the considerations of the people who worked at Federal Plaza. They were also very serious people, who responded to Serra's airy conceptions with the substantial reality of their experience. Middlebrow culture had once existed as a conductive medium between artist and audience. With the *Tilted Arc* controversy, it became clear that middlebrow culture in America had disappeared once and for all. Serious art became art understood as such only by a privileged few. It became "serious" art.

Meanwhile, there were the falling tax rates. Until 1982, the top marginal tax rate in America was always between 63 and 92 percent. From 1944 to 1963—the decades of intellectual seriousness we just described—the top marginal rate remained between 91 and 92 percent. In 1982, it fell from 70 to 50 percent, and in

1987, it dropped to 28 percent. During this time, payroll taxes increased, and more and more tax breaks were ended, but the former increase hit the middle class, and the effect of the latter was canceled out by the wild proliferation of tax shelters. I don't like high taxes any more than anyone else does, and I have no argument about tax policy. I simply wish to point out that surplus wealth created an atmosphere in which money had the last word over culture.

Because some works of art and some books made stratospheric profits, gallery owners, art dealers, and book publishers began to expect every work of art and every book to make lots of money. The publishers of serious magazines harbored the same expectation. After a while, a serious poet or composer couldn't afford to rent an apartment in New York, that center of seriousness; after a while, apartments could not be rented at all, but only bought at exorbitant prices. The economy became so revved up, so many people became rich, and so many other people became so unimaginably rich that anything that didn't seem profitable didn't seem serious. Seriousness without wealth began to seem quaint. Seriousness with wealth began to seem less serious than just plain wealth. The economic structures that had supported a freelance intellectual life dried up. The intellectual was replaced by the well-remunerated academic whose seriousness seemed less organic than institutionally derived. The reality of seriousness became replaced by the legendary reputation of seriousness. The scare quotes began to grow.

Another development in the transformation of American seriousness had occurred earlier than the radical tax cuts in the 1980s. The Vietnam War had made the politician seem silly in his patent dishonesty. The politician had once been a statesman, a paragon of seriousness: FDR, Truman, Eisenhower, Kennedy, Proxmire, Dirksen, Fulbright, Moynihan. Now it was clear, beyond all doubt, that the politicians who had led the country into the war with North Vietnam, or had stood by while the war raged, had either been lying or guilty of bad faith. The baton of seriousness passed from the politicians to the journalists who had exposed them.

With the help of large amounts of capital, the media became the foremost arena of seriousness. At the same time, the academics who had taken over the serious function of the intellectuals turned themselves into media celebrities. One of the only old-fashioned intellectuals to become a media celebrity, Norman Mailer, once wrote that the television camera seeks out the emptiness in its subjects. If you said anything complex, the camera would fall asleep and refuse to make you come alive. The problem for the new academic celebrities was that the camera can titillate and shock, but it cannot deal with seriousness.

It came to pass that art and literature, once able to astonish people with new aesthetic forms and provocative social commentary, were surpassed by the media's minute-by-minute novelty and transgressiveness. The serious journalist—Walter Cronkite, for example—trained as a newsman, began to be displaced by the performer, the "talking head" with no body of experience under it. Serious journalists, like Cronkite, had to start learning how to perform for the camera as well.

Again, it was Sontag who had foreseen this. She had prescribed "theatricality" as a way to go beyond what she called "straight seriousness." She had seen theatricality as the bracing new wave of anti-serious seriousness. But the powerful new media had immediately formalized theatricality. The newscasters began to take their role as performers more seriously than what they were performing. It wasn't long before the audience began to take them lightly as a result. *Saturday Night Live* mocked television journalists the way *Rowan & Martin's Laugh-In* had once mocked politicians. The idea was to sock it to seriousness whenever it raised its head, since you knew that it was, by the simple fact of its public presentation, insincere.

In the meantime, the acceleration of the money culture was creating the Internet in its own image. Even more than the Internet's attacks on every type of seriousness that had the slightest whiff of authority behind it; even more than its wild creation of every type of silly diversion; even more than its celebration of silly enraged opinion over considered, serious judgment—even more than all these novel developments, the Internet took on the character of money's leveling neutrality. Like money, the Internet has no morality. Neither does radio or television or any technology, of course, but no other communication technology possesses the Internet's simultaneity of countless moral, immoral, and amoral functions. Just as money can be used for an infinite number of purposes, so can the Internet. The indiscriminateness of the medium, the instantaneity of it, the miraculous convenience of it, strike seriousness dumb.

But, it was the Iraq War that delivered the coup de grâce to a stable contemporary seriousness. The revelation that Saddam Hussein did not have the weapons of mass destruction that the broadcast and print journalists said he had was fatal. Fairly or not, it discredited the entire media the way Vietnam had once discredited the entire political establishment. The serious journalist who had displaced the serious politician lost his stature. He joined the serious intellectual who had been replaced by the serious academic—who had then been trivialized by the blandishments of celebrity culture. The old forms of seriousness withered away, yet to be replaced by new ones.

That was when the comedians took on the mantle of contemporary seriousness. When in 2004 Jon Stewart went on CNN's *Crossfire* and accused CNN political commentator Tucker Carlson to his face of, in effect, not being serious enough, people responded with manic enthusiasm. When, more recently, Stewart ripped into Congress for not passing the 9/11 First Responders Bill—legislation that would pay for treatment of illnesses contracted by the first responders to the Twin Towers after the attacks—people spoke about the rebirth of serious journalism, even though authentically serious journalists and commentators had been ripping into Congress for the same reason. When, in 2006, Stephen Colbert upbraided a startled President George W. Bush as the guest comedian at a White House Correspondents' dinner, the media's first response was chilly indifference to Colbert, but it didn't take long before people started speaking about him as though he were Gandhi—even though authentically serious public people had been excoriating Bush for years. There was something touching yet also pathetic and absurd about such desperate inflation of comics to the status of intellectual saints. It revealed an impatience with the inability of official seriousness to get things done. It expressed a wish for the timeless pendular motion of seriousness versus anti-serious seriousness to swing into the latter phase.

The die had been cast long before. Once the earlier exemplars of seriousness, the politicians, journalists, and academics, became clowns, the professional clowns who exposed the former's silliness took their place. Laughter—negative seriousness—ruled. But there was no complementary, positive seriousness to complete it.

For better and for worse, Jon Stewart, by far the most serious and consequential comedian around, plays a prominent role in the pages that follow, which explore the status of seriousness in culture today. You will also encounter some of the polished makers of a contemporary image of seriousness, and you will meet one academic-cum-intellectual whose impersonation of seriousness has the effect of both sustaining it and diminishing it. You will be introduced to the humiliation of a serious writer—Updike—who had been around too long, as well as to the ossifying of the serious genre he worked in. You will read about a new style of seriousness, and about a type of seriousness that is nothing but an elitist's defensive posture. You will learn about the fate of the intellectuals in an age where the ultimate questions seem to be economic ones. And you will learn what makes Oprah a supremely successful hybrid of seriousness and silliness.

But comedy, the strange, new contemporary comedy of antic gravitas, is at the center of it all. Despite the complexity of its nature—the comedian's supreme aim, like the politician's, is to please his audience—the new comedy's laughs are like the howls of labor, as a new wave of seriousness struggles to be born.

Capturing the Predicament of Seriousness

We want to be focused and to have a sense of continuity in our lives. We wish to possess the force of purpose. Yet so much stands in our way. The technology of entertainment makes us dreamers. It tempts us to live vicariously through the lives of celebrities. It makes us constantly wonder who we are by offering us the chance to be countless other people.

The most serious artists of our time have made our dreamy, vicarious nature the subject of their art. One of the best of these, Elizabeth Peyton, is redefining what it means to paint a serious portrait. In doing so, she is redefining what it means to be serious, period.

Peyton portrays historical figures and celebrities she has never met—Napoleon, King Ludwig of Bavaria, John Lennon, Kurt Cobain, and Sid Vicious—as people she knows intimately. And she depicts her close friends—aspiring bohemians from the East Village and East London—with perplexingly vacant faces, in moods of mysterious yearning. The juxtaposition of famous and obscure is the psychological crux of her art.

Peyton is a highly literate painter whose book-size paintings, done mostly in oil, initially promise an intimacy with her subjects. Yet here is the twist: the more closely you look at her work, the less intimate your experience of it becomes.

Consider her 1996 oil portrait of *Piotr*. A twentyish blond man sits relaxing in a chair, gazing outward, holding an empty cup in one hand, his other arm resting on his leg. But he is not entirely at ease—there is a slight stiffness around his shoulders and his neck. The painting radiates ambiguity. As is typical of a Peyton subject, Piotr holds an elusive gaze: he could be studying something or someone in front of him, daydreaming, or sinking emotionally behind an empty stare.

The painting evokes an uneasy psychological atmosphere, yet its vivid colors belie its unsettled mood. Piotr wears a button-down reddish-orange shirt that subtly blazes against a crimson background. And his hair is undergoing some kind of metamorphosis from red into gold, like that of a young god.

You suddenly realize that you are not experiencing a person, but a puzzle woven around a person, a social and psychological riddle that is also made up of art-historical allusions, from Antoine Watteau's wistful youths to Pierre Bonnard's haunting ellipses. This is not so much the image of a person as a person's ideal image of himself.

Most of us have fairly straightforward expectations of serious portraiture. We feel that the painted representation of a person should capture something of his inner life, his character and personality—think of Rembrandt's or Eakins's faces, human atlases of particular fates and circumstances. The master portraits of the past have even led us to expect some indication of the subject's position in society. But like historical styles of seriousness, as we have seen, the portrait has undergone countless revolutions since its realist perfections in the Renaissance and then during the Romantic and early Modern periods. Peyton's work is the most interesting recent upheaval of the genre.

For one thing—with rare exceptions—it was not until relatively recent times that painters started to portray friends, or strangers, from ordinary walks of life, using their names to identify them. For centuries, the purpose of depicting another human being was to represent a historical, mythical, or biblical exemplar of virtue or vice; or to pay homage to the subject's social status (usually he was compensating the artist for the privilege of being immortalized); or to record an anonymous social type: Rembrandt's *The Jewish Bride*, Gustave Courbet's *The Stone Breakers*, et cetera.

It was in the Romantic period that the definition of serious portraiture began radically to become something else. Painters began to paint individuals simply because they were (often nonpaying) friends or acquaintances. These were usually other artists or writers—Delacroix's portrait of Chopin, for example. Only at the threshold of Modernism did you get anything like portraits of an artist's friends from other professions—a doctor or lawyer here, an influential art-dealer everywhere. Not to mention mistresses and lovers.

The introduction of the camera instigated another change. As photography progressed, people could be portrayed not just as social types but as individuals with names and contexts. (Consider Lewis Hine's 1908 photograph *Sadie Pfeifer, a Cotton Mill Spinner.*) Eventually, the speedy, accurate, portable Leica became to the portrait what representative democracy was to the nation-state. Now portraitists did not just have carte blanche to capture anyone they wished with their brush and palette. In order to compete with the camera's populism, they had no choice but to paint people from all walks of life.

And with the ascendancy of the camera came the rise of what we refer to now as "the media." This wreaked the greatest change of all on the portrait.

It was one thing for Rembrandt—or Titian, or Vermeer, or Van Gogh, or Whistler—to capture the inner life of his subjects on a single canvas. The uniqueness of the work of art seemed to correspond to the uniqueness of the life depicted by the artist. Looking at the timeless portraits of the past, you feel as though you are in intimate communion with the people portrayed, as though it is your own intuition that is grasping the subject's essence.

It is quite another thing for that illusion of complete knowability to be reproduced on a mass scale and projected in newspapers and magazines, on the silver screen, on the small screen, on the screen of your smartphone. Engulfed in mass media's sometimes blinding visual clamor, the beautiful illusion of intimate knowability all but dissolves away. How can an individual's delicate, intricate inner life be grasped by the entire world? That is to say, how can inner life, once the keystone of artistic seriousness, be portrayed in contemporary terms?

As Modernism picked up speed at the beginning of the twentieth century, artists set about reclaiming an individual's fullness of complexity by making the face almost impossible to see. Radical experimenters like Picasso broke the human figure up until it was almost unrecognizable. Adventures in reconfiguring the human face continued well into the 1950s, when Abstract Expressionist painters like Willem de Kooning rang the final changes on that tradition, though with some irony. Much of the purpose behind the many Modernist distortions of the face was, simply, to shatter the formulaic media images of people and to recapture the mystery of being a person.

Beginning in the 1960s, and especially in this country, a realistic style began to reassert itself. People like Alex Katz, Alfred Leslie, and Chuck Close were creating paintings that reached back into painting's grand realist phases—from the flat visages, rendered without perspective, of ancient Rome (Katz) to Van Eyck's clinical precision (Close). Painters hungered to reclaim the face, as if in life-and-death competition with the Hollywood close-up. Peyton's languid, vague, almost sticklike figures—somewhere between painting and illustration—are the latest, original phase of fifty years of American artistic wrestling with the human face in the teeth of photography, movies, television, and now the Internet.

Sleeping, reclining, sitting, daydreaming, fantasizing, brooding—Peyton seldom depicts these young artists and musicians standing, and she almost never visually associates them with an activity like making art or music—Peyton's friends and lovers Piotr and Tony encounter her celebrity obsessions John Lennon and Prince Harry and Kurt Cobain like chess pieces on opposite sides of existence. Those in the tribe of the obscure look strikingly similar to one another: blank-faced, thin, closed-up yet strangely open, looking so intensely outward that it feels they must actually be looking inward.

They are also strikingly similar to the tribe of celebrities, who bear the same physical features. You feel that the desire of Peyton's friends to be famous is so powerful that they have acquired the appearance of the celebrities they yearn for—the way dogs begin to resemble their masters.

But nearly all of Peyton's subjects, both famous and obscure, don't just resemble each other. They also look a lot like her: delicately featured, wispy, androgynous. Peyton has spoken of how moved she has been by Marcel Proust's meditations on the nature of time, and of how Proust's novel has influenced her attempts to capture her subjects in the web of fleeting mortality. But it seems that what she has really taken from Proust is his exploration of the way we project ourselves onto the objects of our desire. We re-create the people we love—and the people we hate—in our own image.

Peyton's likenesses may not capture her subjects as intimately as we would like, but she has used the embattled genre of portraiture to lay bare a very contemporary perceptual and emotional predicament. At a moment when technology has made it possible to "know" people without ever meeting them in the flesh, there is the peril of imagining them as mere reflections of our own wishes and obsessions. Then, too, we have just lived through a time when we were tempted into projecting our desires—some would say our greed—onto reality beyond the point where they could ever be satisfied. Most of all, Peyton has captured the simultaneity of public and private lives, rather than being overwhelmed by it. She has allowed us to contemplate, with the utmost seriousness, some of the contemporary obstacles to attaining it.

Making Seriousness

Yet one person's struggle for seriousness is another person's opportunity. Culture abhors a vacuum every bit as much as nature does. I have on my shelf a first edition of Garry Wills's *Bare Ruined Choirs*, a 1972 book of essays that examined the role of prophecy and social commitment in a declining Roman Catholic Church. In his photo for the book, a bespectacled Wills is sitting in a backyard or park, his shirt open and his sleeves rolled up, two pens clipped to a slightly sagging shirt pocket, the author looking off to the side with almost embarrassing eagerness—he might be waiting to be invited to mix it up with the other boys. The camera has ineptly caught just one dimple and, on the other side of Wills's face, what is either a long sideburn or one half of a straplike beard unaccompanied by a matching mustache. The picture is charming, though its subject might just as well be an early software engineer or a polymath cabdriver. That indeterminate relationship between appearance and reality is what makes it charming.

Eleven years later, Wills appeared in another author photograph. What a difference! No cluttered yard-type scene here. No untethered details like that droopy shirt pocket, or that eager look. And no doubt that this is a Serious Writer. This time, Wills sits inside, on a broad wooden armchair with upholstered back and seat. Wearing his by now trademark large-frame glasses, he is posed like a statue under a window, which is off to his left, just above his shoulder and only partly visible. So transparently staged is the photograph that Wills's shadow is not cast by the light through the window. Rather, it falls on the wall beneath the window, thrown there by some mysterious light source beyond the picture's border, somewhere on Wills's right. The strangest thing is that a shadow also appears on the right side of Wills's face. That would be pretty much impossible if the source of light creating his shadow on the wall were also on his right.

Wills holds his hands clasped in his lap and stares into the distance. Unlike the earlier picture, though, he doesn't seem to be looking at anything. His face is like those ancient busts with blank spots for eyes; it's been wiped clean of the earlier photo's spontaneous animation. Subject and environment are under the total control of the photographer. The composition exudes gravity, enigma, formal beauty, perfection—and exceptionalness, as if time itself had stopped to look at the person sitting in that chair. This aura of utter isolated mysterious originality is, we are being told, what it means to be an exemplar of Literary Seriousness.

Marion Ettlinger, who took that picture of Wills, is probably the most sought-after book-jacket photographer in the country. She's been snapping authors for more than twenty years, coming to prominence in 1983, when *Esquire* sent her across America to take pictures of nearly fifty writers. Since that time, this gifted figure has become the photographer of choice for publishers mindful of a culture where fame provides the most effective commercial allure, and where the authority of a beautiful and perfect appearance constitutes the essence of fame. Her name has even entered the language as a verb. To be "Ettlingered" means to have imparted to you an aura of seriousness, distinction, and renown, regardless of whether anyone besides your mother and your cat knows who you are. In the marketplace, where despite the Internet and its deluge of images, books must still be bought and sold, and profits made and authors paid, Ettlinger's camera is to a writer what Pierce Brosnan is to an Omega watch.

Before the advent of Ettlinger, authors often tended to appear on the covers of their books in relaxed, unself-conscious moods and settings, a style that publishers now seem to consider an inadequate rival to the flawless images purveyed by fashion, movies, and television. The appearance of fame has become indispensable to the impression of seriousness.

Ettlinger is indeed doing portraits. Yet these portraits serve the purpose of book-jacket photos, and this gulf between what her photographs are and what they are actually doing is part of Ettlinger's innovation. Ordinarily, a portrait's function is to have no function except the representation of the subject. Julia Margaret Cameron's celebrated photographs of Alfred Tennyson and Thomas Carlyle are portraits. So are Berenice Abbott's iconic pictures of James Joyce. The subjects of those pictures acquired, through their work—or through titanic expectation that became a kind of original work itself—reputations that had become larger than their writing. Serious labor preceded and justified the appearance of seriousness. Thus their images could acceptably appear independent of a dust jacket.

Ettlinger's pictures, however, are made expressly to adorn book jackets. Their function is to be, as it were, purely functional—informative, curiosity-satisfying. They are absolutely dependent on the publication of the book, which is a one-time event. The two masterpieces in Ettlinger's book *Author Photo* are the pictures of Truman Capote and Harold Brodkey, both of whom had accrued reputations, as a result of serious work, that were permanent events beyond the occasion of a book.

There is, then, a quality of displacement in Ettlinger's work. Her photos are made for the cover of a book but aspire to the glory of a wall. Perhaps this disjunction reflects the strangeness of conferring the illusion of fame upon people who are not yet accomplished enough to be famous.

Like her overreaching photographs, and her transparently avid subjects, Ettlinger herself seems to want something more than to work as the momentary employee of a publisher in the service of an author. I can't think of another book-jacket photographer whose style is as immediately recognizable as Ettlinger's. It is almost proprietary. She often uses the same wood chair, or similar-looking ones, as a prop for her authors, and likewise a wood table. These are not just Serious, or Serious-Looking, writers; they are the Serious creations of Marion Ettlinger, Serious photographer of the Serious. The chair and table, the immortal stillness, the cinematic excitement, the shrewd assimilation of glamour to literary precincts—these are Ettlinger's trademarks. They are like the designer labels on clothes.

And one wonders whether what seem to be Ettlinger's worthy ambitions for herself don't have a constricting effect on her subjects. Here are these (supposedly) inward, introspective, idiosyncratic, socially fairly useless writers who spend their solitary lives trying to go their own way, so that they can set beside society's official big picture their own original, peculiar, created worlds—so that they can often puncture official seriousness with good old pendular anti-serious seriousness. Then the masterful Ettlinger comes along—or, to be precise, is invited along—and casts these creatures of their own imaginations into tightly controlled environments, hands them props and asks them sometimes to wear costumes, and requests that they pose in such a way as to accomplish the picture's formal aspirations. Writers whose daily struggle is to relinquish their egos are made intensely self-conscious about their vocations and their looks; people who spend their time peeking behind appearances are reduced to appearances. As Richard Ford—one of Ettlinger's most handsome, and interesting, and mysterious-looking subjects—effusively puts it in his introduction to *Author Photo*, Ettlinger's pictures are "averrals that the pictured author of the book you hold in your hand . . . is a person handsome, interesting, dramatic, weird, friendly, mysterious, possibly even forbidding enough to have written something you simply won't be able to put down."

You don't know whether to laugh or cry when you read that inversion of a once-unthinking assumption that appearances don't add up to reality. Here is an author beseeching you to judge his books precisely by their covers! Here, in the name of seriousness, is seriousness turned utterly upside down and inside out.

The Last Serious Intellectual?

At this late date in our American civilization, seriousness has numerous caricatures. Ettlinger can "do" seriousness to a fare-thee-well. So can George Steiner.

Back before the economic meltdown, the nanosecond news cycle, and our surprise-a-minute public life replaced reflection with the necessity of just keeping up, people argued about the merits of this fabled literary scholar, critic, essayist, amateur linguist, and amateur philosopher as if they were debating the fate of culture in modern life. In fact, they were doing exactly that.

Steiner has poured forth millions of words on the fate of art and literature in modern times. His central obsession is the Holocaust, and specifically the haunting fact that the Holocaust's ashes spread from high culture's Promethean fire: the civilization that produced Bach also produced Buchenwald. In books like *Language and Silence, In Bluebeard's Castle, After Babel, Real Presences*, and in countless magazine essays, Steiner both celebrated culture's survival and questioned its value in an age of atrocity and disbelief. These are, as Matthew Arnold would agree, subjects of high seriousness. But Steiner's provocative lifelong inquiry into the sources of human cruelty and creation does not alone account for his controversial status.

Born in France to an Austrian Jewish family that escaped Vienna, Steiner has had a life that is like a textbook definition of seriousness. He was raised in Paris and New York, and educated at the University of Chicago and Harvard, and then at Oxford. He taught at Cambridge for several years, then accepted a professorship at the University of Geneva. After that, he shuttled back and forth between prestigious universities here and in England before retiring from teaching. All the while, he published dozens of critical monographs, a handful of novels, and hundreds of essays, articles, and reviews.

Steiner aroused his share of outrage with his passionate aversion to Zionism, and especially with his 1981 novel *The Portage to San*

Cristóbal of A.H., whose portrayal of Hitler (playfully presumed to have survived the Second World War and been spirited by his supporters to South America) some readers thought strangely sympathetic. But even more than these brief uproars, what once made Steiner such a contested figure was the question of just what type of bearer and interrogator of high culture he was. Celebrated as a one-man bastion of high Western culture and admired for his moral subtlety by some, Steiner was attacked as pompous, pretentious, and inaccurate in scholarly matters by others. His bracing virtue has been his ability to move from Pythagoras through Aristotle and Dante to Nietzsche and Tolstoy in a single paragraph. His irritating vice has been that he can move from Pythagoras through Aristotle and Dante to Nietzsche and Tolstoy in a single paragraph.

Is Steiner the Last Serious Intellectual? Or a comforting caricature of same? Someone you can read in a fit of inattention, purposelessness, and discontinuity, yet still feel, you know, serioused-up?

Absurdly or gratuitously pedantic comparisons flow from Steiner's pen like impersonations of high seriousness: "More, perhaps, than anyone since Nietzsche and Tolstoy . . ."; "Like Pascal, like Kierkegaard and like Nietzsche . . ."; "In a way and on a scale inconceivable to Western man from, say, Erasmus to Woodrow Wilson." He has a flair for portentous statement of the obvious: "Massacres have punctuated the millennia with strident monotony." He also has a flair for portentous statement of the obscure: "The shade of a shadow . . ."; "The political-social desideratum . . ." The grating hallmark of his prose is an almost self-parodic knowingness: he will make allusions without explaining the reference and allude to events without describing what happened. Sometimes it seems that for all of Steiner's vaunted erudition, he is so intellectually ambitious that he frequently feels insecure about his command of the material under review, and overcompensates with a flustered stream of cultural name-dropping. His editors were perhaps too insecure to intervene.

Yet a spiritual energy has enlivened Steiner's work, drawing in readers who surrendered themselves to his profligate ruminations. He has attributed this quality to Arthur Koestler, who, he wrote, "seemed to exemplify Nietzsche's insight that there is in men and women a motivation stronger even than love or hatred or fear. It is that of being interested—in a body of knowledge, in a problem, in a hobby, in tomorrow's newspaper." An intensity of outward attention—interest, curiosity, healthy obsession—is Steiner's version of God's grace. There is something both exalted and wonderfully mundane about that.

To put it bluntly: Did Steiner present art and ideas as the organic urgencies that they are—did he bring out the *ser* in seriousness? Or did culture become for him—as it does for certain people—simply an extension of ego, a one-man kingdom, the keys to which he flaunted and jingled under the reader's nose while he solemnly pranced back and forth, reciting names of the distinguished dead as though they were aliases for himself? Was he, in his need to impress and win the favor of his audience with his bravura performance of seriousness, merely silly?

Since Steiner's erudite voice grew more authoritative the more he published, the George Steiner problem came to encompass the larger question of just how culture gets transmitted.

In his polymorphous, polymathic, polyglot—he has taught in four languages, and knows many more—attraction to just about everything under the sun, Steiner resembled that other great explicator of culture to the matriculated masses, one of our exemplars of cultural seriousness, Susan Sontag. They both were critics of the open-minded school, mostly generous in their judgments, abundant in their generalizations about life beyond the subject at hand. But in the deeper sense, Steiner was everything Sontag wasn't—and vice versa. He was the anti-Sontag.

Both critics made their careers introducing and explicating major trends in European culture to Americans, but the ironic contrasts between them are rich. Though Sontag published in highfalutin journals like *Partisan Review* and the *New York Review of Books*, she expounded radically democratic notions of pleasure and power. Steiner, on the other hand, used the solidly middlebrow *New Yorker* (or the equally bourgeois *Times Literary Supplement* in Britain) to examine and ultimately uphold the sacredness of the very high culture Sontag was attempting to deflate. Both writers, consciously or not, appealed to their audience's vanity: Sontag allowed her intellectually aristocratic readers to indulge their contempt for middle-class Kultur, while Steiner enabled his middle-class readers to feel empowered by aristocratic ideas of truth and beauty.

At the same time, again and again, in essays on Bertolt Brecht, Bertrand Russell, Alexander Solzhenitsyn, Céline, Anthony Blunt, Simone Weil, Steiner likes to take on complex personalities, double-sided genius-monsters. "Where are the bridges in the labyrinth of that soul?" he asks about Céline, the brilliant novelist and vicious anti-Semite. About the xenophobic Solzhenitsyn: "This colossus of a man, so markedly a stranger to common humanity." On the pacifist Bertrand Russell's nearly homicidal cold-heartedness: "Bertrand Russell is a man who loves truth or the lucid statement of a possible truth better than he does individual human beings."

Reciting such elegant moral conundrums has been Steiner's way of easing the general reader into culture and then out again. Out of the Promethean fire comes destruction: if you have time to apply yourself to the treasures of Western culture, fine; if not, count your blessings. At the core of Steiner's horror that the instruments of civilization—language and even rationality itself—are also the weapons of barbarism is a palliative for the harried reader's conscience. You haven't finished Proust's novel? Being good, or at least not monstrous, is even better. Steiner efficiently offered one double-sided solution to the problem of preserving your attachment to culture after the long leisureliness of college. He has kept people interested in the world of literature and ideas, and he has freed them from feeling guilt when their interest flags.

In that sense, Steiner was indispensable as the bridge between Arnoldian seriousness and what used to be known as middle-brow seriousness. Indeed, his star rose as the status of those other former conduits between middlebrow and high culture—the academics—began to become ever more obscure.

Academia in America passed through three stages. First was the philological stage, from the nineteenth century up to the Second World War, when classicists and bibliographic scholars existed in rarefied seclusion, devoted to parsing etymologies and establishing the authenticity of texts. Then came the freelance, or public-intellectual, stage, when middlebrow and high culture seemed most comfortable with each other. That was when literary critics and even novelists who wrote for mass publications flooded the postwar universities as professors and instructors. Finally, there was the theoretical stage, when academia once again became as exclusive and professionalized as it had been during the philological era, but now with an emphasis on esoteric European theories and radical political posturing. The theories endeared the new philologists to a chic downtown crowd, a position that for a few years propelled some of them into the lap of a media hungry for the edgy and the hip. And the semblance of radical politics made them attractive to a media hungry for protest against what liberals considered the oppressions of the Reagan era. By 9/11, however, the theories had become irrelevant to a volatile new world, and the politics seemed disengaged from political reality.

Steiner maintained echoes of all three academic phases—his classical erudition, his accessibility in the pages of popular magazines, his occasional denseness and tantalizing obscurity. He was also, at the same time, a necessary semi-caricature of those true paragons of seriousness, the American intellectuals. Do you remember the intellectuals? There has recently been a sea change in the status of these at times noble and quixotic animals. They have been orphaned by circumstance. Those traditional arbiters of what is serious and what is not have become extinct. The economic crisis has forced a massive layoff of the intellectuals.

When the *New York Times Magazine* describes Newt Gingrich as "a prospector in bold and counterintuitive thinking—floating ideas throughout his career," you know the word "idea" has wandered, as if in a drunken stupor, far from its original connotation. CNN senior political analyst Gloria Borger struggled to adapt to the new meaning, whatever it is: "The problem with Gingrich is that he has fabulous ideas."

It used to be that when intellectuals heard the word "derivative," they thought about what Marx took from Hegel. Now they clutch their heads in confusion and despair. Arguments about small versus big government used to entail reflections on the nature of man and society, the question of balancing the highest good against the greatest number of people who might benefit from that good, the meaning of power and of authority. Not anymore.

These days, just about every political debate comes down to one phrase: economic policy. Occasionally, things grow more specialized, and just as intellectual disputes over class conflict once spilled over into philosophical differences over "dialectical" change, the issues of taxes and spending branch out into the exciting topic of "earmarks." Sometimes things get fancy: you might hear the term "moral hazard." But just when the intellectual wheels start to turn—Aristotle's *Ethics*! William James's pragmatism! Sartre's existentialism!—you realize that you've eavesdropped on a conversation between an insurance broker and a management consultant about the proper way to structure a transaction.

What we never hear about in the popular media—where intellectual discussion sometimes took place—is debate over fundamental meanings, or essential definitions, or connections between seemingly unrelated phenomena. Those are the elements of an idea, which is the challenge consciousness makes to concrete reality. Those are the basic lineaments of the old seriousness in its varying degrees, from Socrates to Matthew Arnold to Robert Maynard Hutchins to Allen Ginsberg to Susan Sontag. When Archimedes said, "Give me a lever that is long enough . . . and I will move the world," he was talking about how you can think your way into a new actuality.

Instead of ideas, we have "issues," which are the way the world tricks consciousness into believing that things never really change. Because an issue has two sides to it, both sides will still be there, whichever one prevails. The "issue"—consider abortion—never goes away. But an idea—e.g., the issue of abortion is more fundamentally about the social limits of sexual pleasure, not merely about reproductive rights—leaps beyond the two sides of an issue into the essential condition from which they spring. It makes you stop to think, instead of provoking you to start to argue. An issue should lead to ideas. Instead, issues are often the place where ideas run out of steam, and where seriousness becomes crowd-pleasing silliness.

As a result of our yapping, endlessly banal, issue-dominated culture, the intellectuals who work with ideas the way a realtor works with property, are out of work. No wonder we are surrounded by the Rush Limbaughs, and the Donald Trumps, and the Jim Cramers, the buffoon-priests of silliness who preside over the ongoing national game of issue ping-pong. Lacking ideas to grab our attention and make us focus, the intellectuals have given way to ranters, abusers, and screamers, who have the effect of both grabbing our attention and freeing us from having to pay attention.

Of course, no one should blame the intellectuals for not being able to grasp our fathomless economic mess. An old joke went that only two people in history understood Hegel, and even they misunderstood him. Well, the only people who understand the present constantly evolving crisis are economists and tax lawyers. And even they misunderstand it. I have heard tales of award-winning poets and novelists nearly reduced to tears trying to comprehend the relationship between mortgage-backed securities and recession.

Still, the question remains whether we are really the worse off because of the superannuation of ideas and of the people who have them. Not necessarily. Seriousness requires a goodness of purpose. An idea and the capacity to have one are not inherently good.

Ideas drove the various responses to the economic calamities of the 1920s—the result was totalitarian ideologies on the Left and the Right and the annihilation of tens of millions of people, all in the name of one idea or another. The Cold War, as we noted earlier, provoked an incredible intellectual ferment, not just in political rumination but in every area of culture, from the postwar novel to Abstract Expressionism, yet that conceptually heated atmosphere also created paranoia across the political spectrum, as well as an endless cycle of payback and score settling. And the rifts produced by the idea-besotted sixties continue to bedevil us.

The poet William Butler Yeats might have been right when he wrote that "an intellectual hatred is the worst." We, on the other hand, are not in the grip of inflexible principles and unwavering obsessions; we are not motivated by unexamined emotional wounds that have disguised themselves as ideas. We (extremists not included) apply ourselves to the facts as they arise, with a (relative) minimum of conceptual bias. That does not seem to have made our public life less polarized, but at least it is keeping it peaceful and (historically speaking) civil.

There are dangers, though, that accompany our idea-impoverished condition. Ideas don't just make sense of reality; they keep our perception of it clear. With the intellectuals off the job, gross distortions of our condition and its broader context may well multiply.

Now that the intellectuals are on the unemployment line along with everyone else, too much of what used to be known as false consciousness is going to slip into people's unsuspecting minds, like pollutants into reservoirs. For months, while the economy was slipping backward, the phrase du jour, used by people throughout business and media, was "moving forward." As in: "Dear Employees, Moving forward, we are laying off several thousand of you." And the dishonest, weaselish phrase kept advancing, with no one to stop it. Language like that is a lubricant to the calamity all around us.

If nothing else, intellectuals, who are compulsive scrutinizers and falsehood-exposers, console us for our troubles by blowing the whistle on just such petty insults to our dignity. Their abstract models of what ought to be instead of what is even sometimes inch reality a little closer to becoming bearable. But their particular subdivision in the industry of seriousness has, for the moment, been shut down. Even George Steiner would have nothing to say about derivatives.

Unmaking Seriousness: How Fiction Lost Its Serious Edge

When seriousness becomes a self-conscious style, formulated like a recipe and marketed by book-jacket photographers, it is open season on the real thing.

Gandhi once famously described the four stages of nonviolent protest: "First they ignore you, then they laugh at you, then they fight you, then you win." John Updike experienced something like the same phases of response to his work—true art is nonviolent protest, after all—but in reverse. One of the most serious American novelists who ever lived was turned utterly upside down and inside out and made to appear silly.

Amid the routine homages to Updike that appeared after his death in 2009, at the age of seventy-six, one fact was almost entirely airbrushed out of his life. This astonishingly gifted and creatively vital writer, who started to seriously work out his destiny in his work at the age of twenty-two, when *The New Yorker* bought a story and a poem that he had submitted; who received two Pulitzers, two National Book Awards, and four National Book Critics Circle Awards; whose enormous body of work had earned him global recognition—this literary genius had, by the end of his career, become either a target of ridicule or been forgotten by literary culture altogether.

Strangely, it was the vital constituents of Updike's seriousness—his remarkable productivity, his graphomaniacal compulsion to annotate every lush detail of existence—that had been one of his detractors' chief grievances.

"Has the son of a bitch ever had one unpublished thought?" David Foster Wallace nastily imagined readers "under 40" asking about Updike, in a 1997 essay. Updike's most tireless persecutor, the book reviewer James Wood, was less colloquial but more cutting: "It seems to be easier for John Updike to stifle a yawn than to refrain from writing a book," Wood wrote in 2001.

No serious American novelist with Updike's accomplishments has ever been treated with as much disrespect as the author of the Rabbit tetralogy and dozens of other books. A few of Updike's characters—Rabbit; the Maple family; Updike's unlikely alter ego, sad-sack Jewish writer Henry Bech—have become part of American folklore. Yet he was not just attacked. He was abused.

People reacted to Updike's plentiful writings—23 novels, 146 *New Yorker* stories along with more than 500 reviews and poems, dozens of humor pieces, gemlike art criticism in the *New York Review of Books*—with something like angry contempt, as if his prodigious publishing on diverse subjects were not the serious force of creative nature that it was, but some kind of Ponzi scheme directed at sucker readers. Just before Updike's death, an editor of the *Los Angeles Times Book Review* publicly implored Updike to publish less, surmising that "perhaps there'd be more room at the bigger publishers" for "writers who are doing exciting things."

During the past decade or so, the negative responses to Updike were devoid of the respect due to a person, let alone an artist of Updike's caliber. In that same several-thousand-word essay from 1997, Wallace quoted a friend who insulted Updike with adolescent verve as "just a penis with a thesaurus." Recently, the novelist Nicole Krauss offered a sharper judgment: Updike was "an old fart." Harold Bloom sniffed him away as "a minor novelist with a major style."

But it was James Wood who opened the floodgates for Updike hatred. No critic had ever come at Updike so relentlessly, viciously, and articulately as Wood. After Wood began to draw blood, it was open season. Updike's detractors had to inflate their vitriol just to keep up.

From almost the time he started to work at *The New Republic* in the midnineties, Wood began writing about Updike as if making slashing comments on a student's midterm exam. The two-time Pulitzer Prize winner wrote prose that suffered from "a professionalized ordinariness," whatever that meant. Updike actually published in airline magazines, Wood mocked. Updike's language "lifts itself up on pretty hydraulics." His entire body of work was "not only dated, but provincial and minor." Wood concluded that "Updike is not, I think, a great writer." And why was this? "Because Updike is unable to picture a reality more powerful than his own. He is unable to picture the opposite of his own reality."

So much for the hyper-delicate, exquisite, Proustian sensibility that created Rabbit Angstrom, the former high school basketball star, kitchen-gadget and car salesman, afflicted so powerfully and convincingly by tragedies and failures that never touched Updike's own starry life. Not to mention Henry Bech, an urban Jewish novelist as "opposite" to Updike as Anna Karenina was to Tolstoy.

When *The New Yorker*, which had been Updike's home since he was in his early twenties—to the point where both magazine and writer were almost synonymous with each other—hired Wood in 2007, it was hard to imagine that Updike did not experience it as a brutal judgment of his current worth.

Updike's close association with *The New Yorker* was, in fact, a Faustian bargain that both made his career and obscured his inestimable value as a literary artist. The relationship was a study in the need for seriousness to keep itself from being institutionalized in order to stay fresh. No major American novelist has ever been so intimately identified with a magazine. In an issue of *The New Yorker* largely devoted to Updike, which was published after his death, critic Adam Gopnik wrote that Updike "took, and kept, a tone" from the magazine, which was the "White-cum-Thurber sound of the *New Yorker* . . . that . . . lingered in his work till the very end."

What *The New Yorker* bestowed upon the humbly born, stuttering, psoriasis-afflicted young man from the Pennsylvania provinces was a loyal and lucrative home, prestige, glamour, and all the gilt-edged trappings and hidden entitlements of the literary life: the entrée to privileged circles; the rarefied imprimatur that gave him an edge in literary competition, and also provided him with a special connection to Knopf, the country's most powerful publishing imprint; and the magazine's hallowed, sheltering mystique.

What Updike surrendered in return was the popular image of the novelist as an unaffiliated, independent free agent, uninflected by institutional influences or pressures, whose writing was unalloyed by a collective "tone" or "sound." His comfortable identification with *The New Yorker* robbed Updike's seriousness of its organic quality.

Of course, plenty of other reasons exist for the special spleen directed at Updike. There were his middle-class, suburban, frankly Protestant settings, which made modernist Jewish critics like Harold Bloom see red. When Updike defended his decision to support the Vietnam War twenty years earlier, in an essay he published in 1989 in *Commentary*—the by then neoconservative headquarters of Jewish intellectual modernism—he must have known that he was opening a hitherto locked door.

Then there was Updike's 1986 speech at the PEN conference that year. As Norman Mailer and others thundered against the oppressive state, Updike slyly celebrated America's singularity in the form of a modest tale about a reliable postman delivering to Updike uncensored mail. Updike's 2006 speech at the Book Expo convention in Washington, D.C., in which he predicted the death of the author and the book at the hands of Google and the Internet's "electronic anthill," marginalized him even further.

But it was Updike's Dorian Gray–like relationship with *The New Yorker* that finally determined his ludicrously unfair treatment by the literary establishment. He was not, in people's stereotype-laden minds, a novelist confronting life's elements and ordering them out of his own guts, guile, and gift. He was not a sovereignly autonomous Hemingway, or Mailer, or Roth. He was, in the end, a *"New Yorker* writer." The fabled magazine both gave Updike his renown and explained it away.

When the institution rotated on the axis of its need and

brought into its fold Updike's toxic foe—the type of cuts the comparatively mediocre Wood made are like poison to a writer's ego and will—it was not being malicious, or personal. It was being an institution. And Updike, whose fiction concerns men seeking a home in a world where mortality sweeps all stability away, stayed in what had been the warmest and most protective of homes.

The American cultural inflation-deflation machine being what it is, Updike can always be re-serioused. Americans love closure, after all, but hate finality. As the narrator writes in Updike's immortal story "A Sense of Shelter," about an adolescent who has an epiphany about life's transience: "Between now and the happy future predicted for him he had nothing, almost literally nothing, to do."

What cannot be returned to its original vitality is Updike's chosen medium: fiction. It was hard not to recognize in the contempt directed at Updike a displaced unhappiness with the novel's own status—a frustrated novelist himself, Wood had made one published attempt at the form that was a resounding flop. Updike had not only been the victim of longevity, one of seriousness's most merciless foes. He was the victim of the gradual de-seriousing of his form of art. The novel is coming dangerously close to outliving its function.

Try this experiment. Ask yourself if the novel is still culturally relevant. Then ask yourself when the last time was that you read a novel that moved you the way film moves you. Be honest. Now ask your friends. Of course the novel is culturally relevant, they will say. Then ask them the same question about the last novel they read. What did I tell you? About a year ago, I posed that question in print and received a storm of impassioned protest in response. You would think that if the novel's relevance and health were self-evident, it would not be necessary to respond—and to respond with such emotion—to an argument that it wasn't. It seemed that I was on to something.

A novel for the ages can still be written. Memorable stories, long and short, continue to be created. Jonathan Franzen's novel *Freedom* was on everyone's lips after it was published, as people gratifyingly argued about his representation of American society, culture, and politics. Franzen's book was indeed a serious work of art, and without a doubt, the next male or female Hemingway, Faulkner, or Fitzgerald is also out there somewhere, hard at work. But with the exception of a few ambitious—and obsessively competitive—fiction writers and their agents and editors, no one goes to a current novel or story for the ineffable private and public illuminations fiction once provided. Franzen's novel was forgotten in about two weeks. Yet people are still talking about films like *Avatar, The Hurt Locker,* and *The Squid and the Whale.* The furious critical attention that Franzen's novel received was almost heroic. It was a self-created and self-sustaining attempt to make the novel as culturally relevant as a movie once again. It had the sad effect of proving the novel's waning relevance.

Urgency and intensity were the feelings with which people used to respond to novels by Updike, Roth, Cheever, Malamud, Bellow, Mailer, Ellison, Styron, Vonnegut, Hardwick, Fowles, Didion, Heller, Capote—the list goes on and on. Mary McCarthy's *The Group* was a bestseller, and a critical success, and a scandal, and a book read by "civilians"—i.e., not just aspiring fiction writers who read other writers the way doctors read professional journals and lawyers keep up with the law reviews. But, then, in those postwar decades, there was another sign of how central fiction was to people's lives. So-called commercial fiction was just as relevant to people's lives as so-called literary fiction. Herman Wouk's *The Winds of War*, James Jones's *From Here to Eternity*, Chaim Potok's *The Chosen*, Harper Lee's *To Kill a Mockingbird*, Marjorie Kellogg's *Tell Me That You Love Me, Junie Moon*—these novels were all what was called commercial fiction as opposed to literary fiction, but they mattered to people. They captured the ordinary events of ordinary lives, and they were as primal as the storyteller singing around the pre-Homeric fire. Now nearly everything literary is also furtively commercial, but almost none of it is popular, except for the explicitly commercial fiction that the literary crowd refuses (or is unable) to write.

Alas, the practice of fiction has become a profession, and professions are not characterized by originality. The carefulness and cautiousness of professionalism is what is keeping contemporary fiction from being meaningful to the most intellectually engaged people. Fiction has now become a museum-piece genre most of whose practitioners are more like cripplingly self-conscious curators or theoreticians than writers.

There are other forces eroding the immediacy and intimacy of the novel, too. We are self-absorbed to a degree perhaps unknown to humankind. This makes it hard for writers to evoke other people and their physical environment. It also makes it hard for readers to be interested in any type of characterization or description that they cannot vicariously inhabit. And language itself has become degraded: This sucks. OMG. WTF. LOL. NSFW. You're a douchebag. This kind of coarseness and abbreviation makes literary language all the more defensive and self-consciously "literary."

Surrounded by our gadgets, we have also lost the knack for the solitude that serious reading and writing once required. Between the previous paragraph and this one, I checked my e-mail, clicked on the weather report, read a friend's Twitter feed, and Googled "train sets" (for my son). As a result of our dependency on the technology of information and communication, even the most literary among us use language almost exclusively to communicate rather than to capture, analyze, or evoke.

Finally, we are becoming more visual and even musical than we are verbal. We are seriously visual and musical, but few of us any longer are serious readers.

For all the negative effects of seductive new technologies, even more destructive to the novel was the rise of critics who saw themselves as composing exegeses of fiction that surpassed fiction itself in their creative power. When Harold Bloom brilliantly transplanted all of Western literature to a claustrophobic Freudian realm in which "texts" responded in a spirit of Oedipal rivalry to other "texts," he was projecting his own wish to murder the artist and replace him or her with Bloom the critic. There was a time when literary critics—Edmund Wilson, Alfred Kazin, Irving Howe, Lionel Trilling, Diana Trilling, F. W. Dupee,

Elizabeth Hardwick—used criticism to connect books to the social, cultural, and political life around them. Starting in the 1970s, critics like Bloom, and later others, such as Paul de Man and Stanley Fish, worked to reposition literature as being relevant only to theories about literature. Without the vibrant interaction between critics, novelists, and a mass audience, the novel—the first serious form of mass art—had its days numbered.

Still, it is unfair to blame a relative handful of American academics from the 1970s onward for the slow death of the novel as a living form of seriousness. Before high academic theory, there was the killing hand of a theoretician whose ideas quickly became modern society's new framework of seriousness: Sigmund Freud. Freud was a plague on the novel.

Freud's ideas spelled the death of psychology in fiction. His abstract, impersonal concepts slowly wore away the specificity of fictional character. By the 1950s, here and in Western Europe, it was making less and less sense to fashion the idiosyncratic, original inner and outer lives of a character in a novel. His or her behavior was already accounted for by the universal realities of id, ego, superego, not to mention the forces of repression, displacement, and neurosis. For all the rich work published after the war, there's barely a fictional figure that has the memorableness of a Gatsby, a Nick Adams, a Baron de Charlus, a Leopold Bloom, a Settembrini. And that's leaving aside the magnificent nineteenth century, when authors plumbed the depths of the human mind with something on the order of clairvoyance. Of course, before that, there was Shakespeare. And Cervantes. And Dante. And . . .

It seems that the further back you go in time, away from Freud, the deeper the psychological portraits you encounter in literary art. Nowadays, often even the most accomplished novels offer characters that are little more than flat, ghostly reflections of real people. The author's voice, or self-consciousness about voice, substitutes mere eccentricity for an imaginative surrender to another life.

The everyday familiarity of Freud's ideas has created a totally psychologized culture. We are so used to talking about people's inner lives and motivations that it has become almost impossible for a novelist to plumb the inside of a character's mind without sounding parodic or banal. When the novel reached the height of its relevance and power, from the mid-nineteenth century to the early part of the twentieth century, public talk about sexual motives and drives, about the most intimate desires, was nonexistent. The framework for artistic seriousness has changed.

The Making of a New Seriousness

Do you remember when we said that, throughout history, vigorous types of seriousness become old and give way to a new wave of seriousness? In the decline of the novel, we are seeing that phenomenon with our very eyes.

If we have Freud to blame for the long-drawn-out extinction of literary character, we also have Freud to thank for the prestige of film. The depiction of fictional people's inner lives is not the strength of the silver screen. Character gets revealed to us by plot turns, camera angles, musical scores—by abstract, impersonal forces, much like Freud's concepts. In a novel, character is shaped from the inside out; in a film, it's molded from the outside and stays outside.

How many movie characters can you think of—with the exception, perhaps, of Charles Foster Kane—whose names have the archetypal particularity of Jay Gatsby or Theodore Dreiser's Sister Carrie? For better or for worse, film's independence from character is the reason it has replaced the novel as the dominant art form in our culture. Lately, however, this independence of character has become a reinvention of artistic character. The rise of intelligent animation is having the ironic effect of making film more literary.

Pixar is to contemporary seriousness what, in the late nineteenth century, Dickens was to literary seriousness. *Finding Nemo* and *The Incredibles*—to take my two favorite Pixar films—are not so much visual works as visual candidates for the occupation of a literary void. One reason audiences flock to these and other animated films is that they would rather experience cartoon figures who operate with complex psychologies than unachieved literary characters who act like cartoons. When we disparage a poorly developed character in a novel by calling him a "cartoon," we are saying that he is too general and abstract to be believable as a person. But the generality of a complicatedly scripted animated figure has the reverse effect. As the character deepens from type into a concrete figure, symbolic and specific meanings fuse. Novelists have become increasingly self-conscious about psychological categories. Cartoons, however, offer an evocative externality. The viewer supplies the interiority himself—out of his own.

Disney was making animated movies long before Pixar. But

a wide gulf exists between the old and the new animation. It is because of Disney that we think of animated movies as children's fare, yet Pixar's roots are in the more sophisticated tradition of DC and Marvel comics. Buried in the dual nature of the comic book creation of Clark Kent/Superman is a provocative contest between superior human qualities and the ordinary virtues of democratic man—"Superman" was where Nietzsche tussled with Walt Whitman.

Pixar was born more from such playful insinuations than from make-believe Disney "magic." It brought mainstream, commercial animated film into the literary realm. *The Incredibles* is a story about superheroes who have to hide their powers in order to avoid the envy and resentment of their fellow citizens. It is both a nod to Superman's hidden dilemma and a winking commentary on the limits of our so-called meritocracy. That's about as far from Mickey, Donald, and Co. as you can get.

Pixar's success at making intelligent cartoons is a seminal moment in the culture. American life is so crazy-quilted that animation's figures—these symbolic particularities—might be the only way to encompass not only the way we live but also thoughts and feelings that have become lost to us in all the mad velocity we are surrounded by.

Pixar's creations have a lot to teach novelists, too. They might start with *Finding Nemo*—that fairy-tale-like story about the death of a mother, the loss of a home, the cruelty of the outside world (and the occasional kindnesses that make the cruelty both easier and even harder to bear), and a father's and son's search for each other. Yes, they're fish. But the Greek gods who transformed themselves into animals, and the Greek poets who invented those transformations, did so in order to refresh the imagination by slipping into something a little less comfortable and a little more strange. Intelligent cartoons are yet another powerful form of imaginative refreshment.

Faux-serious Urban Snobbery?

Pixar's new seriousness recalls the seriousness that characterized educated taste after the Second World War. In its emphasis on finding stability in a hurtling world, Pixar has more than a touch of that old middlebrow, middle-class seriousness. Nemo and his father live, for all intents and purposes, in a watery suburb. That would immediately brand them as unserious in today's precincts of serious taste.

For urban cognoscenti, seriousness is defined by the spires and canyons of urban environments. For this tribe of people, environment is destiny. A life in the suburbs dooms you, not only to emptiness and lack of meaning. It sentences you to death by silliness.

Consider the movie adaptation of *Revolutionary Road*, based on Richard Yates's 1961 novel of the same name. It is the latest entry in a long stream of art that portrays the American suburbs as the physical correlative to spiritual and mental triviality.

The movie's opening scene could serve as a précis of over fifty years of anti-suburban sentiment in American culture. Frank and April Wheeler pull their car over to the side of the road. They've been fighting, and now they both jump out into the dark of the night. When April's needling escalates to downright cruelty, Frank pulls back his arm as if to hit his wife and then slams his fist into the car. She's been tormenting him, he cries, "ever since we came out here to the suburbs."

In the naturalistic novels of Émile Zola, Stephen Crane, and Theodore Dreiser, economic forces inexorably destroyed the protagonists. In *Revolutionary Road*, the two principal characters are brought down by lawn sprinklers and station wagons.

But Sam Mendes, the film's director, is just getting started. Flashbacks emphasize the chilling role the tortured couple's environment has played in the disintegration of their lives: against a background of sunlit, leafy yards, we see Kate Winslet taking out the garbage, Kate Winslet doing the laundry, Kate Winslet making small talk with a neighbor. The treelined streets are empty and eerily quiet. The beautiful house is tastefully furnished and eerily quiet. You are meant to think of the Wheelers' suburb as "a place where one can ruin oneself, go mad or commit a crime," to borrow Van Gogh's description of an equally alienating milieu (except that Van Gogh was talking about an urban café).

Still, the film's hostility toward the suburbs pales when compared with its source. Yates's novel, cherished by serious literary intellectuals to this day, expresses American suburbophobia with crude explicitness. Describing the Wheelers' new neighborhood, Yates writes: "The Revolutionary Hill Estates had not been designed to accommodate a tragedy. . . . [The neighborhood] was invincibly cheerful, a toyland of white and pastel houses whose bright, uncurtained windows winked blandly through a dappling of green and yellow leaves. . . . A man running down these streets in desperate grief was indecently out of place."

No literary critic that I know of has ever challenged Yates's puerile social perceptions. The reflexive reverence for *Revolutionary Road* is a testament to the degree to which anti-suburban sentiment is one of the serious literary elite's most unexamined attitudes. For what might a neighborhood that had been designed to accommodate a tragedy possibly look like? For a man running down the street in desperate grief to fit right into the landscape, he would have to be hurtling through a place where vampiric towers blocked out the sun and corpses hung from the lampposts.

Yates's rage against the suburbs had all the subtlety of adolescent rage against authority. This indiscriminate anger might account for the novel's fatal deficiency: Frank's and April's total lack of talent or substance makes their ultimately thwarted attempt to leave the suburbs for Paris less the stuff of tragedy than irritating farce. Yet *Revolutionary Road*—the name fatuously meant to imply that America's revolutionary promise withers and dies in the suburbs—caught the reflexive attitudes of many readers. Postwar writers and intellectuals overlooked the book's flagrant shortcomings, lit up from within by their shared opposition to a single place. X might be a Stalinist, and Y a fellow traveler, and Z a closet Republican, but they could all agree on one thing—they'd rather perish in a nuclear holocaust than move to Westchester! The serious framework of the cultural elite has no room for the serious framework of a life like that of Jackson, our hypothetical artist turned suburban husband and father.

American anti-suburban sentiment is often comically absurd.

In his 1955 poem "Howl," Allen Ginsberg elevated suburbopho-bia to the level of myth. He excoriates the "invisible suburbs"—i.e., they are so spiritually dead that they are hidden from a living eye—as one of the pernicious manifestations of Moloch, the de-structive god of soulless materialism. (Ginsberg was at his most silly when trying to be serious.) Sylvia Plath added some spine-tingling details. In her 1963 autobiographical novel, *The Bell Jar*, Plath's heroine steps off a train and has this infernal experience: "The motherly breath of the suburbs enfolded me. It smelt of lawn sprinklers and station wagons and dogs and babies. A sum-mer calm laid its soothing hand over everything, like death." The pleasures of a station wagon's aroma are open to question, but summer calm, the smell of wet grass, the scent of dogs (if they're clean) and babies (clean or dirty) are, it could be argued, some of the least horrifying experiences in life.

For Yates, Plath, Ginsberg, and less gifted suburbophobes such as the novelists Sloan Wilson and John Keats, as well as hugely influential liberal sociologists and writers, such as David Ries-man, William H. Whyte, Paul Goodman, and Betty Friedan, it went without saying that the suburbs could transform the people who had committed the error of moving to them into the walk-ing—make that driving—dead.

Yet the Wheelers live in a safe and protected middle-class town with intact, well-to-do families; efficient services; and happy chil-dren gamboling in sprinklers and running among the trees. Like Jackson, our ex-painter, they are serious people who live serious lives of devotion and commitment. How did such an environment come to acquire qualities previously associated with Dante's *Inferno*, Dickens's Victorian workhouses, and Solzhenitsyn's gulags? How did the "wrong" locale become the very emblem of silliness in the eyes of official seriousness?

In the fifties and early sixties, the postwar exodus from the cities to the suburbs was just beginning. Veterans of the Second World War and then the Korean War sought inexpensive homes of their own, far from the urban scrimmage that must have been, for some, a cramped extension of real combat. Enterprising builders eagerly obliged, throwing up houses in a matter of months, modest Cape Cods and ranches that returning veterans were able to safely buy with little or no down payment, thanks to the GI Bill.

It's easy to see why artists and intellectuals felt that they had to alert the general public to the emergency of these sudden new places' peaceful, leafy streets. For one thing, the suburbs seemed not to offer the primary experiences of either country or city. The backyard is but the reminder of a meadow; the treelined intersection is but the faint echo of a busy urban intersection. The suburbs were the embodiment of that period's fashionable existential fear: "inauthenticity."

More important, suburban houses were often designed along unsightly cookie-cutter lines. The archetypal suburb, Levittown on New York's Long Island, was constructed between 1947 and 1951 using assembly-line methods; at one point, thirty houses were springing up every day. In 1950, when builder William Levitt, who created Levittown, appeared on the cover of *Time* magazine, the conversation in the cafés of Greenwich Village must have sizzled with frightening visions of totalitarian sameness. And, no doubt, the suburbs as brainless utopias devoted to silly pursuits, as they were depicted on the television sitcoms of the time—shows like *Leave It to Beaver, Bewitched, Father Knows Best, The Dick Van Dyke Show*—also incited intellectual revulsion, as much against the sinister new mass medium of TV as against the suburbs themselves.

But there were two overarching reasons for condemning the suburbs, during the fifties and early sixties, as the most rotten place in civilized life: class and money. These are two of the most powerful shaping influences on seriousness, and they do their work in secret. Most of the people leaving the cities for the suburbs in the 1950s were tradespeople, modest businessmen, teachers, and the like. They were members of the middle class, the impassioned rejection of which has been the chief *rite de passage* of the modern American artist and intellectual. With the growth of suburban towns, the liberal American intellectual now had a concrete geography to house his acute sense of outrage.

Yet if the suburbs were becoming the headquarters of the American middle class, they were also becoming associated with the enviable characteristics of upward mobility: a decent salary, home ownership, access to superior public education and services. "We're going to have to move back to the city," the callous but suddenly redeemed advertising man grimly says to his wife after quitting his job in disgust in the popular 1959 film *The Last Angry Man*—moving from suburban Connecticut to hardscrabble

Manhattan being proof of his redemption. What a socioeconomic difference fifty years makes.

Art and intellect are solitary vocations, and their practitioners often require a common enemy to sustain the lonely effort. The suburbs continued to serve that purpose, but the type of antipathy toward them changed in the late sixties and seventies.

In the Vietnam-era, artists and intellectuals grew impatient with aesthetic and intellectual considerations. Now the suburbs were stigmatized not only by materialism, lack of imagination, and conformity. From that moment—and up to our own—the suburbs were portrayed in every type of art as noncommunities that signified ugly moral choices.

The cultural chasm between liberals and conservatives that first appeared in the sixties was largely one between the city and the suburbs. The liberal "idealism" that had created the catastrophe in Vietnam now got blamed, unfairly or not, for failing economic and social policies. For marginalized conservatives, the suburbs were living refutation of the crumbling ethos that had guided the crime-ridden, decaying urban centers. For embattled liberals, people leaving the cities for safer and cleaner outlying towns were racists and cowards who had no respect for shared public space. In this respect, Richard Serra's *Tilted Arc* posed a taunting challenge to the mostly suburban commuters forced to experience it: You think you can come into the city every day and experience in Federal Plaza the solipsistic illusion of security you have in your leafy towns? Think again. Yet one of the most glaring ironies of American life is that, a quarter-century later, the cities have metamorphosed into the suburbs—sans trees and grass. The cities' storied diversity has devolved into global chain stores. The bottle of electrolyte-enhanced water and the branded baseball cap have become the accessories of a universal comfort and conformity. As we have noted elsewhere, in a social and cultural sea change, the cities' rented apartments, once the guarantor of diversity and fluid, exciting movement, have been converted into exclusive co-ops and condominiums.

As the cities have become a new type of suburb, suburbophobia has become an ever more acceptable cultural attitude. The suburban person is considered too meek, too asphalt-challenged, and thus too unserious to inherit the earth. In the urban centers, on the other hand, desperate ambition makes bad manners respectable, and the chic of perverse taste covers up Philistine cluelessness. The decent suburban person is regarded as contemptible because he has not learned to reach beyond his talents and pick life's pockets. In urban eyes, the open pursuit of money, power, and fame is considered the sign of an ultimately serious approach to life.

In the last couple of decades, the anti-suburban film has become as much a staple of Hollywood as the Serious Crime Drama with an Incomprehensible Plot. A few prominent examples: Todd Haynes's *Safe* (which has suburban people inexplicably bleeding from every pore of their bodies); the 2004 remake of *The Stepford Wives* (where Viking range + Sub-Zero refrigerator = robotic wife, death of feminism, and extinction of human rights); *The Ice Storm* (just in case you ignored the urgent alarm sounded by the anti-suburban novel, on which the film is based, and moved to Larchmont); the British Sam Mendes's very own *American Beauty* (of which *Revolutionary Road* is simply a reiteration—take a sprinkler, add a dollop of anomie, and presto! you're an authentic American filmmaker). Television, once home to the idealistic vision of the suburbs, has gotten in on the act, too, with the anti-suburban satires *Desperate Housewives* and *Weeds*, not to mention the Real Housewives franchise, which opens a fake-appalled window onto a world of midday margaritas and $18,000 sleepover parties.

It could be that suburbophobia has been a necessary attitude for ex-suburbanites living in urban centers. It may well help them to feel that the increasingly anodyne and homogenous cities are still adventurous and challenging places to live. In any case, suburbophobia has even made its way into the visual arts' most rarefied sanctums: in the paintings of Eric Fischl and the photographs of Jeff Wall. One of Wall's most well-known works is his photograph of rifle-holding men stalking an invisible prey in an anonymous suburb.

Of course, there is a small but stubborn countertradition to suburbophobia, most famously in the stories and novels of the much-maligned John Updike and those of John Cheever. For these two writers, the suburbs are not just a determining environment, but an unpredictable one of unfolding circumstances—like every other place on earth. As Johnny Hake, the hero of Cheever's story "The Housebreaker of Shady Hill," puts it: "Shady Hill is, as I say, a *banlieue* and open to criticism by city planners, adventurers and lyric poets, but if you work in the city and have children to raise, I can't think of a better place."

Hake becomes a thief, has something like a nervous break-down, and finally gets an inkling of his surprising destiny. Which only means that life's complexity and surprise, life's seriousness, follow you everywhere, even over the city line, across the river, and into the suburban trees. You wonder why the creators of *Revolutionary Road* are blind to such an obvious fact of human existence.

But, then, Hollywood is the silliest, most illusion-soaked, soul-hardened, and materialistic suburb in the world. Movies are often used to explain society, as if they were mediated yet fairly clear reflections of social experience. Yet behind the movies is a special society, trapped in its particular experience, that explains the movies.

The tacit bargain used to be that working-class and middle-class Americans expected, in exchange for playing by the rules, that the popular culture they turned to for relaxation would reflect back to them positive images of people who played by the rules. Or, at the very least, they wouldn't be made to feel foolish or excluded for dutifully following the rules. The function of a generation of romantic comedies on the silver screen, and sitcoms like *The Honeymooners* or *The Dick Van Dyke Show*, was to ennoble disappointment, limitations, and the postponement—sometimes forever—of gratification. There's scarcely any delay between a wish and its fulfillment in today's movies, where beautiful-looking people are regularly, and graphically, gratifying themselves with other beautiful-looking people. The decline of the sitcom means that the terms of the old tacit bargain are slowly being ignored on the small screen, too, which is an even more consequential development, given that medium's domestic immediacy.

Just think of the political consequences of Hollywood's projection of its own narrow experience into the precious leisure time of its audiences. For many Americans, the promise of instant wealth is a lot more plausible (the market may go your way) than the promise of carnal or romantic gratification (you are who you are). So if Hollywood types, who are nearly all liberal Democrats, are breaking the sexual rules, you might as well go with the Democrats' more regular-seeming rivals. So what if they often seem driven by greed? They are breaking the economic rules as a kind of moral corrective to all the sexual rules—i.e., the tacit bargain—that are being shattered.

As we shall see in later chapters, this chasm between liberal and conservative worldviews is one of the origins of the conflict between red-state seriousness and blue-state seriousness. In the eyes of serious taste, failing to immediately satisfy your desires is the height of unseriousness. And everyone knows that desire thrives in the cities, and goes to the suburbs to die.

In Praise of Folly

Two comedians walk into a bar. One says to the other: "There's nothing like a cold beer on a hot day." The other replies: "It is hard not to be impressed by what seems to be Obama's pragmatic, centrist approach to governing." Ladies and germs, welcome to the new comedy. Or, I should say, the new seriousness.

When Stephen Colbert introduced the term "truthiness" in the debut episode of his show, in October 2005, he said that it connoted an atmosphere in which Americans are "divided between those who think with their head and those who *know* with their *heart*."

There's nothing very comical about making a distinction between rational thinking and the kind of emotionalism that leads to a fanatical outlook. Right or wrong, Colbert is venturing something very serious about American society. It might make you think. It might make you smile. But it doesn't make you laugh out loud. The catharsis comes not from the comedy but from the feeling that reality is being called on the carpet, made to stand stiff with attention, and thoroughly reprimanded like a naughty schoolboy.

Jon Stewart is another master of the reality reprimand. The long list of his errant schoolchildren includes the likes of John Bolton, Madeleine Albright, Howard Dean, and Harry Reid. These figures are not exactly all-star members of team comedy. But Stewart has other uses for them than having them help him churn out laughs, as when he lured Hillary Clinton onto his show the night before the Democratic presidential primaries in Texas and Ohio. Stewart: "Tomorrow is perhaps one of the most important days of your life, and yet you have chosen to spend the night before talking to me. Senator, as a host I'm delighted. As a citizen, frightened." Ba-dee-dum. That was maybe minimally funny. And yet Stewart's sly admonition was bracing, invigorating even, to hear. Senator Clinton's response cut to the core of the matter, too: "It *is* pretty pathetic."

It goes without saying that Stewart and Colbert are often uproarious. But their most memorable shticks aren't shticks at all. Rather, they both utter the type of anti-truthiness truth that never gets said in public. In this sense, they are throwbacks to a humorist like Mark Twain, who was dark, piercing, and wise more than he was simply funny.

Comics like Stewart and Colbert are returning the comedian to the role once played by the court jester, who was allowed to speak truth to power with impunity. Professional fools are spies in the house of power; they can go places few other people can. Recall the Fool confronting King Lear: "Thou shouldst not have been old till thou hadst been wise." Of course, unlike the nonpartisan Fool, Stewart and Colbert have their (mostly) liberal politics, and if you don't share their attitudes, these serious, polemical comedians can seem unbearably knowing and clubby. They can seem the unserious tools of their clique. That is both the annoying limitation and the refreshing gamble of confrontational, interactive comedy. The new seriousness of the comedians shows its cards.

How far we've come from Bob Hope, friend to several presidents, amiably and pleasantly diverting American troops stationed in Southeast Asia during the Vietnam War with innocent one-liners, sing-alongs, and a little cheesecake provided by starlets and seminude young dancers. The routines of Stewart and Colbert are not the reshuffling of familiar experience that has been the stock-in-trade of the standup comic complaining about his wife's cooking or his doctor's cupidity. They are the standup comic telling reality to start behaving, or else.

Modern American comedy begins with standup routines, which reached their peak of perfection after the Second World War. They may well have been called "standup" because they grew out of vaudeville and burlesque, where the humor was as much physical as verbal, and the comics sometimes ended up on the stage, lying down. The postwar standup comic replaced physical pratfalls with an aggressive mentality. Psychoanalysis was becoming mainstream and people were getting used to speaking in monologues to each other as if they were confessing to their doctor. It followed that comedians were feeling more comfortable about talking as though from the couch.

Proclaiming your inner life is an aggressive activity, and this is one reason why standup comedy flourished with middle-class audiences, on the then-burgeoning medium of television, and in vacation spots like the famed Borscht Belt hotels in the Catskills. Such self-assertion was a quality that the growing class of merchants and small businessmen could identify with and laugh at. A one-liner, with its two- or three-part structure, was a kind of transaction—the comedian even "delivers" it, like merchandise— yet one that was liberated from the anxiety and self-consciousness of a real transaction.

But though the middle-class audience could see itself in the standup comic, the comic was separated from the audience by both the stage and by his outrageous conceits or obscenity. Not to mention the segregating formality of the standup comedian's jokes, since laughter in the course of ordinary life doesn't come in the form of a one-liner or a carefully constructed longer joke that is told with expert timing and practiced style. The standup comic was, you might say, an indentured outlaw. He was tied to the audience's approval and largesse, but he existed beyond the audience's respectable pale.

Lenny Bruce changed all that by the early 1960s. His act, as he perfected it, did not depend on the one-liner or on the artfully constructed joke. Bruce told free-form, meandering, improvised stories, some parts of which were funny, some that were mordant or wise, and some that merely baffled the audience. To this day, a lot of people who cherish Bruce's work can't decide whether he was truly funny or not.

Bruce's model was the jazz improvisation. Just as a jazz pianist would take a familiar standard tune—"Autumn Leaves," for example—and then ring changes on it until it was barely recognizable as a standard, Bruce would contrive a comical conceit and make it disappear into an epic tale about life. His monologue "Christ and Moses" wasn't just about the absurdity of the two religious figures suddenly showing up at a Reform synagogue in California and then at St. Patrick's Cathedral in New York (they took a discount flight, stopping over in Chicago), with all the ensuing laughs. It was a sincere and profoundly unfunny meditation—no less—on the true meaning of love and humility, and on the fact that, as Lenny put it, "through usage, [the Bible] has lost impact." Bruce told the story many times. On the recording I recently listened to, the crowd laughed weakly and tentatively, as if Bruce's underlying seriousness was distracting them from his overlying humor.

This was a far cry from the Borscht Belt's indentured outlaws. Even as he was running afoul of the obscenity laws of his day, Bruce was taking the outlaw comedian off the separating stage and blending him into everyday life. Bruce's existential stories were part humor, part auto-therapy, and part wisdom-talking. He might have been someone you met at a bar or party. He might have been a picaresque priest, or a racy rabbi. He might have been you (that is, if you were loosened up by scotch, Valium, and speed). When you listen to old recordings of Bruce and his heirs—George Carlin talking about growing up Irish Catholic, or Bill Cosby weaving a story about driving through San Francisco—you are in a more informal, more intimate relationship with a comedian than any audience ever had with a standup comic.

From the comedian blending into the audience by telling ordinary, often unfunny stories marked by startling insight and truthfulness, it was a short step to what you might call the interactive comedian of today.

The way we watch television is certainly one catalyst for the change. The asocial act of comedy depends on social situations to create an infectious atmosphere of laughter. Even if something isn't funny, an audience of people laughing around you will make you join in. Now more and more people enjoy their comedy by themselves, and they download comedy shows onto their iPods or sneak a procrastinating peek at a streaming video in their office cubicles. But comedy resonates in a different way when you take it in alone. Solitude is a better atmosphere for grievance than it is for knee-slapping hilarity. It also lends itself more to the fantasy of vicarious interaction.

Yet the transformation of the comic bursting with outlaw energy into the reality-reprimander has most to do with society's embrace of the unconscious. Since the sixties, we have seen the hidden secrets of sexual life become media platitudes, the unspeakable become the mundane, the pathological grow into the archly respectable. Consider Hannibal the principled cannibal, or Dexter the virtuous serial killer.

The shocking candor that was once the comedians' stock-in-trade now pours out of a billion public outlets, from Hollywood movies to cable TV to YouTube. At our moment of triumphant uninhibition, figures of even the highest intellectual, or cultural, or political authority seem to lack the discipline and control they are supposed to embody. When respectable society itself becomes asocial, the comedians' reprimands, corrections, and prim admonitions have all the abrasive power of the old outlaw explosions. The old pendular motion still applies. The new seriousness has arrived in the form of the anti-serious.

Jon Stewart: Seriousness as Cool

In January 2010, Jon Stewart caused an uproar when he attacked Keith Olbermann for the latter's "over-the-top" comments about Scott Brown, a Republican who was about to win Edward Kennedy's old Senate seat in Massachusetts. This was a watershed moment in the history of American seriousness.

For about forty years, the public style of seriousness in America had been hurtling through wild permutations. The presentation of seriousness as earnest and authoritative was shot to bits. Gravelly, ultra-sincere seriousness, the seriousness of Walter Cronkite, went the way of discredited authority. Even the earnest and authoritative comedic satirizing of, say, political seriousness—performed by Jack Paar, or Lenny Bruce—became stigmatized. It was generally understood that any public form of seriousness was pompous, absurd, and a mask concealing sinister egotism.

To recap: In the wake of the sixties' upheavals, irony proliferated. It began by blowing smoke rings at authority—George

Carlin, *Rowan & Martin's Laugh-In*, the pre-Postmodern fiction of Donald Barthelme—and finally replaced earnest authority altogether: David Letterman; Comedy Central; the full-blown Postmodern nihilism of David Foster Wallace. Toward the end of the millennium, though, irony itself became a crisis. Irony had grown into the new seriousness. Intended to undermine authority, irony itself had become authoritative. It exerted a coercive pressure: you couldn't be sincere even if sincerity was necessary, because sincerity had been thoroughly marginalized. It wasn't cool to be sincere. But after 9/11, it became clear that it wasn't cool to be ironic, either.

"Cool" (if you will pardon a brief digression) is seriousness's hip cousin. Being cool allows you to circumvent the imperative to never be sincere—but without falling into the trap of reflexive irony.

As term and idea, cool is permanently fixed in American culture. Rarely associated with women (perhaps because, feline and musical as they are, they embody cool's quintessential qualities?), the line of cool runs from Gary Cooper (high cool) to Humphrey Bogart (low cool) to Brando (something of both) through James Dean and Paul Newman and Jack Nicholson and Warren Beatty. Al Pacino and Robert De Niro run too hot to be cool. Even when Brando lost it, he was full of ice. Jackson Pollock was cool on the canvas, but too belligerently drunk to be cool in life. If our Cool Figures are not actors, they're musicians: Miles Davis, John Coltrane, Charlie Parker, Dexter Gordon, Chet Baker, Bill Evans, et al., were, like Pollock, cool only when they were making their art.

Music is the true essence of cool because cool is essentially nonverbal. It either turns language against itself by inventing a new language—Beats and hippies, for example—or stays stone-cold silent.

Cool's various essences seem to be: walking slowly; speaking in a measured, unexcited manner, and usually in a deep voice; treating people who have greater power or authority somewhat haughtily, not to say insolently, while treating people with less power or authority as equals; refusing to act the way other people tell you to act; living unaffected by external forces or circumstances; preferring to be solitary rather than joining the chorus of other people; and speaking in your own original idiom, to the point of even seeming to have your very own vocabulary.

Those qualities are the rudiments of cool. In fact, I've taken them straight out of Aristotle's *Ethics*, where he enumerates them as the defining traits of the "great-souled man," whom we met earlier as the embodiment of moderation and reason. I've also borrowed from Epictetus and Montaigne. You can find similar portrayals of cool throughout Western culture—throughout world culture, actually: quiet, composed Buddha was quintessentially cool—in Machiavelli and in Castiglione's Renaissance guide to being an effective courtier. Cool reached its apotheosis in Enlightenment rationalism, disappeared in Romanticism's raptures, and stayed absent during Modernism's frenzies. It finally surfaced in Postmodernism's hymns to the death of feeling and personality, with the critical exception that Postmodern irony, or any kind of irony, is anathema to profoundly cool people.

For the cool person has no allegiances but possesses an absolute commitment to doing the right thing at the right moment.

Irony has no commitment to anything. In its infinite regression of destructive meanings, irony seems anchored only in the ego of the ironizer. Irony's inability to take a position, to stand by what it says, becomes just as much a concealing mask as seriousness's bluster. For we all know that everyone believes in something, even if it is only the advancement of self-interest.

Cool doesn't pretend not to have self-interest. Rather, it turns self-interest into a gambler's dice. Cool people are quiet people, and cool's orthodoxy of silence means that the cool person is waiting, felinely, to throw his self-interest in the right direction at the right moment. Cool's silence gives it the gravitas of seriousness while seeming to say that it is aware of how deceptive and self-deceptive "serious" language can be. At the same time, cool's silence is a type of piety. It responds to irony's loquacious negativity with the implication of something like faith.

So when the crisis of irony happened, cool—in a fleet new version, adapted to its new moment—was there waiting to usher in a new age of seriousness. We have already mentioned the perverse feeling of cultural gratitude that greeted the attacks on 9/11. Has there been another moment in history when a society's reaction to the murder of innocent thousands of its citizens was a sigh of intellectual relief at the prospect of cultural liberation? In one newspaper after another, happy pundits proclaimed the death of irony. Part of the emotion driving this new sense of freedom from irony was the feeling of mistrust that the ironic atmosphere had given rise to. Mistrust was an intolerable experience following the attacks on 9/11.

After 9/11, being serious and being cool, rather than losing your head, meant the same thing. Seriousness was slowly making its way back, but in the guise of being cool, which now took the form of speaking your mind to what had become hysterical politics—though with intricate variations on sincerity.

From the very beginning of his tenure at *The Daily Show*, Stewart seemed to occupy a position. This became apparent during the second half of his show, when he interviewed prominent figures—at the time, they were mostly politicians—about a book they had recently published. For example, Stewart thanked Richard Clarke, whose book accusing the Bush administration of acting irresponsibly in the war on terror had just appeared, for writing "an eye-opening examination of the true workings of government." For anyone who had either enjoyed or suffered through decades of hip, ironic distancing from any belief or commitment, the experience of seeing this practiced exploder of official position-taking endorse an act of public service was surreal. But there Stewart was, taking a position himself. Stewart was making seriousness cool again. By implication, he was also making it uncool to be entirely negative or ironic.

Of course, like countless agents of serious anti-seriousness before him, Stewart had to put seriousness through some ironic paces. He accompanied his demolition of seriousness with a special caricature. He pretended to be precisely the type of media pundit whose critical seriousness was supposed to see through the serious pose of the politician. His irony attacked in two directions: toward the official political establishment, and toward the official media establishment that had, by the time Stewart started hosting *The Daily Show* in early 1999, become the ascendant cultural activity. Stewart turned the tables on the transgressive, hyper-scrutinizing media and made the media the moral equivalent of sordid politics.

By 2000, this was an easy thing to do. It was widely held, throughout "blue" America, that Bush had stolen the election from Gore (whom liberal pundits had excoriated for appearing . . . too serious) and that the so-called liberal media had let him get away with it. As we have seen, after it was discovered that Saddam Hussein did not possess the weapons of mass destruction that both the political establishment and the media had held up as the reason for invading Iraq, attitudes became reversed. The media that had once, with Watergate and the Pentagon Papers, been synonymous with heroic dissent, now became identified with the very politics it had once taken after with such success.

So Stewart created two types of anti-seriousness that he deployed against two dominant forms of seriousness: politics and its scourge, the media. But the comedian gave his act another twist. Beneath all the hilarious debris, you felt that he was . . . serious.

It was as if, after all Stewart's negations, he had acquired the credibility to modestly put forth something positive. He still interrupted his guests, threw them off balance, mocked those whose politics he clearly didn't share. He always made sure to have the last word. But as his show progressed, he seemed to use the interview with prominent figures not just to score points, but actually to have a conversation. *The Daily Show*'s structure came to resemble *Law and Order*: the first half of the show exposed the criminals and their crimes, while the second half presented some type of rational conversation about "the issues" that wasn't simple mockery and put-downs.

When 9/11 happened—that evening, Stewart seemed to collapse in tears as he spoke about the events of that fateful day—the comedian suddenly seemed to become the representative man of his age. He seemed to grasp the limbo public seriousness had fallen into—the post-Cronkite world, as it were. With his send-up of the media, he was asking a fundamental question: Which was more dangerous, the old world or the new? What is more perilous to our perceptions, a situation in which we feel that news authority is to be taken at its word—thus making us vulnerable to deception? Or a situation in which we feel that the function of the news is to keep stripping away the illusion of its own authority—thus making us vulnerable to the deception that, well, we are now invulnerable to deception? Is it better to have the wool pulled over our eyes, or to be blinded by the illusion of transparency? Better to be deceived as gullible fools, or as knowing fools? Either way, we still keep getting deceived.

Stewart's answer seemed to be to establish a situation in which a new sincerity rose out of the obliteration of the old. Call it preshrunk, distressed seriousness—one that shows its seams and holes only to inspire you with the durability that remains. It was a meta-seriousness, but it was seriousness nonetheless.

Copy, Get Me Seriousness: From Olbermann Doing Cronkite to Cronkite Doing Cronkite to the Post-news Void

Jon Stewart had been hosting *The Daily Show* for over four years when *Countdown* with Keith Olbermann premiered on March 31, 2003. Olbermann's brand of faux-seriousness is a crude variation of Stewart's creative new style. Faux-seriosos like Olbermann (whose multiyear run at MSNBC abruptly ended in early 2011) are always either deliberately parodying or unsuccessfully trying to imitate a particular type of genuine seriousness. Olbermann, the former sportscaster turned self-styled American Sakharov, who did anything to make his niche audience love him, was the very definition of contemporary silliness.

In part, Olbermann fabricated himself as the left-wing answer to that other quintessentially silly pundit Bill O'Reilly, who had been broadcasting from the right-wing network Fox News for several years. Olbermann and O'Reilly needed each other the way seriousness and laughter need each other, though the two of them are devoid of both. Indeed, if in his caricature of seriousness, Olbermann retains a winking insinuation of the countercultural contempt for seriousness, O'Reilly expresses a winking reverence for the high seriousness of the Arnoldian conservatives. At bottom, though, the key to each man's success is the way his performance of seriousness secretly relieves his respective audiences of the necessity to take either of the two men . . . seriously.

But there was a stronger influence on Olbermann than his lucrative pas de deux with O'Reilly. Note the date of Olbermann's first show, which was broadcast just eleven days after the American invasion of Iraq. The effect of Bush and his war on contem-

porary styles of American seriousness is incalculable. The shift
in tone recalls Virginia Woolf's declaration: "On or about De-
cember 1910 human character changed. . . . All human relations
have shifted—those between masters and servants, husbands and
wives, parents and children." The occasion for Woolf's theatrical observation was, so one story goes, the writer Lytton Strachey
running into Virginia and her sister, Vanessa, at a party, pointing
to a stain on Vanessa's dress, and inquiring, "Semen?" Shortly
afterward, Virginia noted in her diary: "With that one word, all
barriers of reticence and reserve went down." By the time of the
U.S. invasion of Iraq, all one needed to do was utter the name
"Bush," and all barriers of reticence, reserve, and also rationality,
came crashing to the ground.

The rise of the political blogosphere introduced an equivalence
between seriousness and invective. Your seriousness increased in
the degree to which you raged and spewed insults. The coarser
and more childish the insults, the more you were perceived to be
maturely committed to a political position. The more friends you
won, too.

Arriving several years after Jon Stewart waxed ironic while
putting irony in its place, Olbermann built on Stewart's innovation. He sharpened and shallowed the irony into sarcasm and
started to make serious political statements from what he clearly
believed was the far Left end of the political spectrum. Then he
gave Stewart's shtick another twist. He adopted the grave, earnest manner of not Walter Cronkite but Edward R. Murrow, that
near-mythical saint of American journalism. Because of his cou-
rageous, on-air debunking of Senator Joseph McCarthy, Murrow

had escaped the stigma that the presidential election of 2000 and the debacle of the Iraq War had attached to Cronkitean solemnity. When you heard Murrow's name, you didn't think of, say, Judith Miller, the *New York Times* reporter who believed fervently that Saddam had nuclear weapons and who became the very face of journalistic complicity with official lies. You thought of Murrow's confrontation with McCarthy at the Army-McCarthy hearings, when Murrow uttered his now legendary words: "Have you no decency, sir, at long last?"

Except that it was Joseph Welch—head counsel for the Army, who was defending it against McCarthy's accusations that it had been infiltrated by Soviet spies—who said those words, not Murrow. Murrow anchored the live broadcast, during which Welch made his ringing cri de coeur. Younger viewers, however, came to associate those words with Murrow, because Olbermann appropriated them one evening in 2006 when he stared at the camera and addressed President Bush: "Have you no decency, sir?" Olbermann sputtered. Just months after the release of *Good Night, and Good Luck*, George Clooney's biopic of Murrow—whose dramatic climax was Murrow's broadcast of the Army-McCarthy hearings—Olbermann seized Murrow's mantle. From then on, he routinely addressed Bush and other political adversaries in his nightly broadcasts, punctuating his accusations and insults with "sir," as if to keep the (false) association of himself with Murrow constantly in his viewers' minds.

Ironically, Murrow himself was thoughtful, nonconfrontational, even morose on the air. He had acquired credibility and popularity with his radio broadcasts from London during the Blitz. In London, he had conveyed through voice alone a sense of urgency, crisis, tragedy, and resilience that he carried over after the war into his presence on the new medium of television. Watching old clips of him on television now, you get a sense of shyness and even reluctance at appearing before the cameras. Cheer seemed to come with some difficulty to Murrow, so when a smile appeared on his face, he seemed spontaneous, boyish, his own forced gesture at sunniness taking him by innocent surprise.

Murrow's gloomy, leaden presence, and his sudden bonhomie that seemed lugged up out of disenchanted yet compassionate depths, comprised an original TV manner. It signaled broadcast seriousness to viewers. After a few years, of course, the original Murrow became "Murrow" and the broadcaster started performing himself, a development that you cannot avoid once you become a public image and begin seeing yourself through other people's eyes. But even this performance of Murrow's stayed within the boundaries of, as it were, the original Murrowness. Viewers were getting a more keenly self-conscious Murrow, but it was not a caricature divorced from real emotion.

With Olbermann, you got an explicit imitation of Murrow, one in which you had no idea what Olbermann himself was really feeling, because he was so thoroughly—and, again, so transparently—inhabiting the legend. Strangely, though, Olbermann's act drew its authenticity from its blatant acknowledgment of its own artificiality. Counterintuitive as it might have seemed to an earlier generation of TV viewers, Olbermann's rip-off of Murrow didn't discredit Olbermann. On the contrary. The very fact that he was archly flaunting his impersonation of Murrow, and thus his unreality as Olbermann, seemed to confer on him just the type of credibility his audience craved.

For the overwhelming fear, washing over the American populace in the wake of the Great Age of Irony, and compounded by the Reign of Bush and the Complicit Media, was that people were not what they appeared to be. The fear was that seriousness had become a manipulative affect. Therefore anyone who came to you professing, up front, not to be what he appeared to be could not be anything but who he really was. The real Olbermann was, clearly, the mass of politically correct sentiments he claimed to be. He couldn't be a phony because . . . he was so ardently, so passionately a fraud! Nor was he trying to put one over on you by attempting to assume the mantle of Murrow's earnestness. His caricature of Murrow—he nearly spit out the word "sir" and at the end of his nightly commentary threw the papers on his desk at the camera—proved that for all of his homage to the mythic newsman, he thought Murrow was a bit of a pompous old ass, too.

Both Stewart and Olbermann used irony to break through irony toward sincerity in the form of invective, finally reaching some sort of plain-spoken sentiment. But whereas the comedian became serious by the end of his show, the serious commentator worked himself up into a sarcastic-comic frenzy by the conclusion of his. Stewart had made it cool to be seriously engaged with society and politics. Olbermann was too hysterically committed to performing committedness to be cool.

So it was, as serious people used to say, "historically inevitable" that one evening Stewart took Olbermann on. It was the great meta-serious face-off. The occasion was Olbermann's tirade against Scott Brown, in which Olbermann called him, among other things, a racist and a homophobe. Though such a train of insults was nothing new for Olbermann, Stewart had his practiced entertainer's eye out for the main chance at upending his sort-of rival, as well as distancing himself from the stigma of being a liberal ideologue, and he pounced. Showing clips of Olbermann's attack on Brown and then commenting on each one in turn, Stewart rose to a surreal crescendo, in which he kept trading one pair of Olbermann's trademark glasses for another, each more outrageous than the next. Finally, he coolly addressed himself to Olbermann. Without lowering the degree of mimicry and Olbermann's own sarcasm, he delivered a serious reproach: "A man of your intellect need not be. Me." Just as Olbermann had become "Olbermann" by performing Cronkite impersonating Murrow, Stewart strengthened his brand by doing Stewart doing Olbermann. He had finished his proximate rival off with a reminder that it was only cool to be serious in a comical context. And once seriousness was vetted and patted down, as it were, by comedy, and then cleared of all pretense and bad faith, it could emerge, checked and double-checked, as itself. Recently, Stewart abandoned comedy altogether by first holding a strangely touchy-feely apolitical political rally in the nation's capital. After that, he spoke out, with Arnoldian absolute sincerity, against Republican opposition to the so-called 9/11 Bill that would grant money to the first-responders at the Twin Towers on that fateful day.

The bill eventually passed, and Stewart was anointed as—who else?—the new Walter Cronkite.

And then it was back to the laugh-a-minute *Daily Show*.

But was Walter Cronkite the touchstone of seriousness in the news? When Cronkite died, one prominent magazine paid homage to him as "the most serious of serious journalists." Yet CBS—Cronkite's old network—praised him for his "serious demeanor." Was looking serious an essential part of Cronkite's seriousness?

The French novelist André Gide once wrote that it was impossible to be sincere and appear sincere at the same time. He was saying that the very expression of an attitude meant that it was being artificially performed. Your appearance of sincerity was, necessarily, the product of an insincere orchestration of sincerity.

We have forgotten that, like his successors, Cronkite was a consummate performer who night after night put the qualities of sincerity and seriousness over on an audience yearning to be authoritatively and avuncularly reassured. Did Cronkite fiddle with his earpiece, or get up and take a look at news as it came in from the wire services, spontaneously? The little scene he performed again and again was meant precisely to convey the unguardedness that is the sign of absolute sincerity, which in turn is the evidence of seriousness. Did Cronkite really break down for a moment as he reported President Kennedy's assassination? Maybe. Maybe not.

Put anyone in front of a camera and they stop being themselves and start being what the camera requires of them. Show someone what they look like in front of the camera and they will never present themselves in the same way again. The difference between print journalism and TV, or what you might call screen journalism, is that the former hides the physical person while the latter reveals it. Once you introduce the element of *watching* someone else, you are in the realm of entertainment. The person you are Skyping with on your computer screen is no longer merely communicating with you. He or she is entertaining you. The advent of the TV anchor is the advent of the journalist as actor. The passage from print to screen also makes it all the more difficult to be serious.

This is not to say that because Cronkite was performing his delivery of the news rather than "being himself" as he delivered it, he was some type of fraud. On the contrary. Our belief in his sincerity is what made him sincere.

What has really changed between Cronkite's heyday and the disappearance of his type is our perception of authority. America and Cronkite both shared the belief that public life did not consist of a series of masks that had to be ripped away. If Cronkite said that's the way it was, then his audience happily believed that's the way it was. We accepted his performance of sincere authority because we wanted to. Believing in his seriousness without feeling anxious about being duped, we believed in the reality of a serious public life.

Now, in their radically various degrees, the Olbermanns, O'Reillys, Stewarts sign off after assuring us that nothing is as it seems. Their job, as different as each figure is from the other, is to puncture anyone who in the previous twenty-four hours told us, with any kind of authority, that this is the way it was. And we happily accept their performance of ironic, sarcastic anti-sincerity because we want to. Yet all we've done is exchange Cronkite's illusion of knowledge acquired (all that's worth knowing is what he told us) for the current illusion of knowingness achieved (all that's worth knowing is that every claim to knowledge is a sham).

It really all comes down to which style of anchor-acting we prefer. Cronkite performed aloofness and detachment. The lachrymose moment in his reporting of Kennedy's assassination was so affecting because he rarely displayed any type of emotion. But even today's network anchors are casual emoters, striving for a kitchen-table intimacy with viewers. As for the cable anchors, their faces are the upper-body equivalent of a failed sphincter nerve. To watch Anderson Cooper mimic happiness, sorrow, anger, compassion, indignation, earnestness in the space of a few minutes—the only element of him that stays jarringly the same is his hip, streamlined, gym-trim physique, as if there were no experience horrendous enough to compete with the perfect workout—is to undergo what the French poet Rimbaud called a "systematic derangement of the senses." Though transformed by the camera, Cronkite performed for an audience. Cooper and his colleagues perform for the camera.

The change from Cronkite's stage acting to today's anchors' film acting is irreversible. Despite all the many laments for the bygone time of reliable news that attended Cronkite's death, it seems that we would not have it any other way. In the days after Cronkite died, we heard, like a mantra, that Cronkite was "the most trusted man in America." The implication was that there has been a terrible falling-off, that the news has let us down and we will never be able to trust anyone like that again.

We were told, over and over again, that although 20 million people still watch the news on the three networks, "trust" will never return, because between 1 and 1.5 million people watch Jon Stewart's skewering of the news on *The Daily Show*. We were told by the very same mainstream media—with peculiar masochism—that college students no longer get their news from newspapers or serious TV news shows, when at no time in modern history did the majority of college students ever show much interest in serious anything, let alone the boring news. Reading the paper or watching the news is part of a routine, and routine comes with age.

If trust ever did return to the news on a Cronkite scale, the media themselves would run it out of town.

Jon Stewart's newfound seriousness will last only as long as it's fresh and surprising. The moment he starts acting sincere on a regular basis, his sincerity will be in danger of being misunderstood as merely an act. Stewart has successfully been able, so far, to walk on the razor-thin edge of sincerity. What he has not been able to do is to seamlessly fuse American seriousness with American unseriousness so that the question of irony versus sincerity becomes moot. Only one public figure has been able to embrace that tension with absolute effectiveness.

Oprah: The Hybrid

There are many reasons for Oprah Winfrey's success, but two stand out. First, she is an uncanny performer. And second, she is half the reflection of her audience's hopes and fears, and half her own creation. Her originality is never so intense that it is something we cannot recognize. And her sincerity is never so pure that we suspect its authenticity. She is a mix of real and unreal, a hybrid of serious and unserious. She is the middle-American answer to Jon Stewart's ironic-sincere, anti-serious seriousness.

The boilerplate criticisms of Oprah are that she exploits a culture of victimization that she did so much to create; she glamorizes misery; she amplifies already widespread self-absorption; she fills people's heads with hackneyed nostrums about life. These criticisms are correct, up to a point. But Oprah's critics write as if her goal of extending to her audience empathy, consolation, and hope were intrinsically cheap and cynical. On the contrary. The question is whether that is really what she is offering.

Oprah's aspiration to inspire her audience with hope—elaborated on her TV show, in her magazine, on her Web site, and now throughout the programming on her very own network—is hardly ignoble. Her "victimized" viewers—not all her viewers, to be sure—are simply people who have been hurt and have nothing to guide them and nowhere to turn. So they make a virtue of necessity and convert their injuries into proactive forces in the world—just as some people turn their old school connections into proactive forces in the world.

Narcissism and solipsism? Sure. But why not call it withdrawal into a protective inner space instead? When Oprah, in the course of seven days, talks to thirteen-year-old boys who have been seduced by their teachers, features "flattering clothes for all figures," presents "five things that can make you younger," and follows that with the story of a woman whose husband set her on fire, she is hitting the different planes of the self like the walls of a solitary fortress. She is one solution to our simultaneity of public and private, to our compartmentalized public life. But she is also the antidote to the media realm in which that compartmentalization is nourished and perfected—the very media realm in which her own compartmentalizations flourish.

The secret of Oprah's television triumph is precisely that her show has been, even amid the recent "reality" craze, the only effective rebuttal to the images of ideal happiness and physique that appear on television. From her first talk show gig in Baltimore hosting *People Are Talking*, in which an overweight, awkward Oprah brought equally ordinary people in front of the cameras to speak with her, she has always thrust life in the face of imperial television. Try to see it in the exalted terms in which her fans regard her: The media is Caesar. Having mastered and then revolutionized its idiom, Oprah is Christ. Like changing water into wine, she has managed—through her elevation of hidden, obscure, or neglected experience into spectacle—to make the television set watch you. Her ongoing battle against obesity was a way for viewers to keep tabs on their own battle against obesity. It was also a remarkable daily progress report on her naked mortality. And thus on yours.

As the culture focused more and more narrowly on personality—on you—Oprah brilliantly expanded her format to put personality at the center of radically diverse experiences. One day, she had physical makeovers (she was almost two decades ahead of shows like *Extreme Makeover*). The next, you "met" a woman who returned home to find her four children shot dead by her ex-husband. After that, a deep commiseration with thin, pale Renée Zellweger over her ordeals with the paparazzi. Then a convening of Oprah's Angel Network, a charitable club that saved enough spare change to send fifty poor kids to college for four years. Or cooking with Paul Newman, or weeping with Sidney Poitier, or hugging Diana Ross. Then a disfigured young victim of a drunk driver meeting with the driver's mother. Followed by "Your Wildest Dreams." And then a psychologist—Dr. Phil for a while, until he started his own show—or a spiritual guru. And then a new book on Oprah's Book Club, almost always about a woman: a neglectful mother, a neglected daughter, an abused wife. Oprah has distilled the total American environment into a unified experience that is accessible to every individual ego.

There's something more, too, something extraordinary. A single week of Oprah takes you from bondage to all the violent terrors of life to an escape through vicarious encounters with celebrity to visions of charity and hope to hard resolve to redemption and moral renovation. And running through these thoughts and sensations is the constant motif—reinforced by self-help gurus—of growth and strength through suffering. Not even fifty years after segregation, America's first black billionaire is offering to her mostly white—if the composition of her studio audience is any indication—female, middle-class audience an astounding experience. She is presenting to them the essential structure of the slave narrative of the antebellum South, right down to her book club's quest for literacy.

The Oprah Winfrey Show is a racial utopia based on the exchangeability of colorless human pain. There is something beautiful and profound about that. As democracy seems more and more to be defined by the number of people who become rich—not many—Oprah's show has gotten more and more popular. In Oprah's universe, democracy is defined by the number of people who are "empowered" by knowing that their sadness and frustration are shared by other people—a lot of other people. It is a kind of egalitarianism from within.

Oprah has said, "If there's a thread running through each show we do, it is the message that 'you are not alone.'" The fluidity of tears represents the essence of Winfrey democracy. We are not alone because we can blur into another person or become another person at any moment. We can make over our appearance, achieve our "wildest dreams," or be heartened by the evidence of charity or by the revelation that the rich and famous are creatures of feeling, too. And if the very worst happened, and we came home to four murdered children, we would know what to expect, having been there, in a way, before. We would not be alone then, either. "Tears, tears, tears! / In the night, in solitude, tears," wrote Walt Whitman, the poet of American democracy. "Moist tears from the eyes of a muffled head; / O who is that ghost? that form in the dark, with tears?" Well, it could be anybody. Almost anybody at all. Oprah has accomplished an amazing trick, or even a miracle: she has turned living vicariously into living authentically.

In other words, she has taken all the forces of silliness in American life and turned them back against themselves. She has turned our fragmentation, and our self-absorption, and the theatrically insincere performance of sincerity that surrounds us into a unique type of anti-serious seriousness. It is unique because she does it without irony, yet still manages to make people believe her. Instead of using irony to signal that she is aware of how "serious" serious has become, she uses weakness, affliction, and imperfection. Whereas Jon Stewart's seriousness lies in the way he can mock or sneer the appearance of "seriousness" away, Oprah weeps it away. Her seriousness lies in the absolute sincerity with which she rises above seriousness to pure feeling—all the while making sure to convey to her audience, to their great relief, that it is all an act, and that the everyday, transactional pursuit of self-interest goes on.

She has also, every bit as much as Socrates, fulfilled her destiny in her work.

The Oprah tale is, as they used to say, a paradigm shift. In place of Horatio Alger's Protestant ethic-driven rags-to-riches story, Oprah's is a Christian fundamentalist–driven tale—by way of the New Age church of self-actualization—of the power of faith and grace. It's not that Oprah hasn't worked hard to get where she is. One of the most appealing things about her has got to be that she always looks exhausted. Oprah has always worked superhumanly hard, it seems, but the object of her work is different from the traditional Alger-type jobs: rag-picking, selling newspapers, et cetera. Oprah's work has been her own life. That is her ministry. She is our watered-down, compromised, half-silly, half-serious TV Socrates.

Oprah has revolutionized the presentation of self on television through the total deployment of every dimension of her life. Her artfulness reached its zenith the very same year that she went public with her tale of sexual abuse. In 1985, she landed the role of Sofia in Steven Spielberg's film of Alice Walker's *The Color Purple*. Like Oprah herself, Sofia was the victim of brutal male abuse. In one stroke, Oprah used her life to capitalize on her role, and she used her role to capitalize on her life. And, by successfully transmuting herself into the fictional character, Oprah could prove to her fans the essential premise of her show: the fungibility of American experience.

But like Oprah herself, Winfreyism has an equally fraught countermotion. Here is where silly comes into the picture.

The reverse side of a democracy based on exchangeable feelings is the creation of a kingdom of mere sensations, in which no experience has a higher—or different—value than any other. We weep and empathize with the self-destructive mother; we weep and empathize with Sidney Poitier; we weep and empathize with the young woman dying of anorexia; we weep and empathize with Teri Hatcher; we weep and empathize with the girl with the disfigured face; we weep and empathize with the grateful recipients of Oprah's gift of a new car to every member of one lucky audience; we weep and empathize with the woman burned beyond recognition by her vicious husband. In the end, like the melting vision of tearing eyes, the situations blur into each other without distinction. The fungibility of feeling is really a reduction of all experience to the effect it has on your own quality of feeling.

In fact, Oprah's universal empathy has an infinite flexibility. When critics complained that she focused too much on stories of physical and emotional horror, Oprah quickly responded, in the early nineties, by mocking that very format. Publicly vowing to start diversifying her show, she immediately incorporated lighter fare more frequently. Several months after Jonathan Franzen dissed her book club, an incident that gave rise to a heated debate over its true function and value, Oprah disbanded it. (It returned, but in a more peripheral and occasional way.) When *Freedom*, Franzen's next novel, came out in 2010, she took care to complete her rapprochement with Franzen and made it a book club choice. (This time, Franzen accepted the blessing without complaint.) The revelation that James Frey, whom she had promoted on her show, had lied in his so-called memoir sent her spinning in appeasement yet again. Oprah's anti-serious seriousness in the form of pure feeling always occurs alongside her silliness in the form of—to be blunt—faking pure feeling for the sake of her audience's love and approval.

One of Oprah's most powerful visual metaphors is how she utterly transforms her appearance—her hairstyle, mode of dress, type of jewelry, even her manner of speaking—from week to week and day to day. It is her clever, dramatic embodiment of the possibility of personal change and growth. But ability to change is also a capacity for accommodation. It hints at a personality that will stretch itself in any rewarding direction, unconstrained by truthfulness or consistency. Unconstrained by the constraint of character, you might say.

The name Oprah gave to her production company—her business—is Harpo Productions, which is "Oprah" spelled backward. That is exactly right. Winfreyism is the expression of an immensely reassuring and inspiring message that has, without doubt, helped millions of people carry on with their lives. It is serious. And it is also an empty, cynical, icily selfish outlook on life that undercuts its own positive energy at every turn. It is silly. (It is sillier by far than the real Harpo, whose farcical muteness bespoke some mysterious pain.) On her way to Auschwitz, sitting in her hotel room in Kraków, thinking about the masses of people who were murdered in the death camp, Oprah wrote in *O* magazine, "I have never felt more human." The uplift she provides her audience seems to require human suffering. Yet watching Oprah does fill you with hope. It also plunges you into despair. She has become something like America itself: struggling to be serious, falling too easily into the morally gratifying shtick of appearing too serious for the sake of being reassuringly silly.

CHAPTER SEVEN

Seriousness in Politics

I was once on a plane returning to the United States from a trip to Russia, where I experienced an illumination of the nature of politicians and politics. As I made my way toward the men's room, I ran into Gary Hart. You remember Gary Hart. A former Democratic senator from Colorado, the married Hart was about to clinch the Democratic nomination for president in 1988 when he was caught in a romantic relationship with a woman named Donna Rice. The Hart affair was the entrance into American politics and culture of private exposé as a tactical public instrument. It was as if catching a politician in a moment of stupidity then threw open the door to a general silliness in the way politics was treated. Gossip and political commentary started to become interchangeable. Hart himself hastened the watershed moment. Responding to rumors of his infidelity just days before they were proved to be true, Hart told the *New York Times*, "Follow me around. I don't care. I'm serious. If anybody wants to put a tail on me, go ahead." Hart helped to redefine seriousness in American politics and journalism.

But it was not Hart's status as an instigator of a new age that enlightened me on that plane. It was his response to me when I introduced myself to him. Having just begun publishing pieces, mostly book reviews in obscure venues, I stretched out my hand, told him my name, and said I was a "journalist." "Ah, yes," he said, smiling at me as if my name had just been on his very lips. Then he shook my hand with surprising firmness, flashed me a second, almost intimate smile meant to reinforce my impression of his familiarity with my work, and moved down the aisle followed by two watchful men who were probably his bodyguards.

Pretending to recognize the name of an obscure writer is a surefire way to win his love. Even after the destruction of his political career, Hart was driven by the need to be loved at all costs. Reflecting on my encounter with him, I eventually realized that if the need to be loved is at the irrational core of the modern democratic politician, then it is at the core of so much of democratic political life.

One of the most formidable pitfalls before seriousness in American political life is not what is conventionally referred to as the "politics of hate." Such a condition certainly exists. But even more consequential is the industry of self-love that has constructed itself, as it were, on the politician's elemental self-love. Even hatred is not enough to make someone pull a trigger. He has to be convinced—such is the power of human vanity—that he is acting out of love for an ideal or a way of life that has been betrayed. An evil person's essential quality is that he takes himself too seriously.

Here is how the twisted politics of self-love works. Phase one: Having said something that wins popular approval, the politician says something else in the same vein, regardless of whether it is rational or justified. Then he will say the same thing, but more strongly, then more extremely. So long as the continuous pumping of that particular sentiment or idea—or ideology or violent emotion—keeps the illusion of love streaming in, the politician will stay with it, flatten it, reduce it, strip it of all nuance and qualification.

Phase two: The individual following this or that political figure acts in the same way. Everybody wants to be loved, and if you find yourself in a situation where one magical sentiment draws other people's admiring attention to you, you will repeat it—regardless of whether it is rational or justified. On the blogs, on the Twitter feeds, on the social-networking pages, the politicized individual coaxes the crowd to his side by using the politician's rhetorical strategy of escalating repetition.

Phase three: Political commentators pursue the crassest partisanship under the smiling guise of objectivity. They hook themselves to an ideological star—all the better if it's a personal star, like that of a president—and become such predictable and reliable promoters of said ideology that they will then be called upon by the media to represent that position. Oh, they still give the appearance of rational detachment and journalistic devotion to the truth. But underneath that they express—I mean, perform—the sectarianism of a Trotskyite operative.

Once these so-called pundits land a berth on a TV show with, say, our two masters of serious unseriousness, Olbermann or O'Reilly, they have to magnify the host's parti pris to keep their position. If they also have access to a print outlet, they will moderate their presence there to preserve print's greater strictness about "objectivity," all the while making sure not to say anything that would compromise, so to speak, their compromised TV personality. In this way, seriousness is parodied as commitment, and commitment is betrayed by opportunism.

In the past, such violent ideological fixity used to be called demagogy, which is the irrational appeal to the emotions. Demagogy was the old anti-seriousness. Now demagogy is the new seriousness. Oprah, as the ruler of a kingdom of interchangeable emotions, is a benign daytime demagogue. Almost forty years ago, the social critic Marshall McLuhan observed that people no longer stayed in one job or relationship, but changed jobs and relationships the way actors go from role to role. "People," he wrote, "are learning show business as an ordinary daily way of survival." Now you might say that when it comes to politics, everyone from politicians and pundits to the ordinary nonpolitician who plays politics on blogs, Web sites, and Twitter is learning demagogy as a daily way of survival.

All this emphatic reiteration of love-starved political rhetoric has two effects. One is to make just about everyone—politicians, pundits, commentators, voters—exaggerate his political "beliefs" to an almost comical degree. (This is why all the comedians need to do to sound funny is repeat what some political or politicized figure has just earnestly said.) The reflexive extremism turns a natural divide in values into a monstrous antagonism.

The other, opposite effect, is to make many people, at some point, and no matter where they are on the political spectrum, sound like their hated adversary. As any student of Nazi Germany and Communist Russia knows, extremes have no place to go but toward each other. Then, too, in our atmosphere of fervent desire to be loved at all costs, the most successful strategy of the other side might as well be yours, too. Especially if you adopt it out of expedience and not commitment, thereby reassuring yourself that you are not betraying your core values. The fundamental silliness of American politics is the fungibility of theatrical extremes—a politics of hate driven by the need to be loved. The larger the divide between the two sides' values, the closer each side's tactics and rhetoric come to resemble the other's. This is not to say that the legislators and statesmen of each side hold morally interchangeable positions. Of course they don't. But the political culture of extremes that bubbles like hot springs beneath the political terrain is the reason each side seems to take the other seriously only as a threat, but never as a legitimate reality.

Seriousness as the Midwife to Silliness

Irving Kristol is routinely described as the "godfather of modern conservatism"—though why he is called godfather rather than father is a mystery: he created neoconservatism; he didn't watch over it. But the description is imprecise in a deeper sense. The intellectually serious Kristol was the father of modern conservative silliness.

An intellectual who constantly put down the vocation of being an intellectual, a gifted wisecracker who reduced complex social problems to glib one-liners—"a neoconservative is a liberal who has been mugged by reality"—a circular reasoner who seemed to care more about the motions of his mind than about the moral or political conclusions he reached, Kristol used thinking to discredit the act of thinking.

In June 1968, Kristol argued that Hubert Humphrey should be president. Several years later, however, there Kristol was, capitalizing on his abrupt turn to the right and enjoying Nixon's hospitality and attention at the White House. It was with voluptuous ease that Kristol had come to a conclusion that was the moral antithesis of his earlier argument for what he had referred to as Humphrey's superior "liberal pragmatism." In the 1968 Humphrey essay, he wrote:

> *The prospect of electing Mr. Nixon depresses me. Suffice it to say that he appeals to the wrong majority to govern the United States in these times—a majority whose dominant temper will be sullenly resentful of the social changes we have been experiencing and impulsively reactionary toward the crises we shall inevitably be enduring.*

Four years later, Nixon's landslide victory perhaps convinced Kristol that this sullenly resentful majority had much to recommend it. It was perhaps the same practical consideration that impelled him to defend McCarthy in 1952, at the height of HUAC's persecutions, when intellectuals, and especially Jewish intellectuals, were generally vilified. For all his caustic polemics, Kristol had an abhorrence of finding himself in the minority. His definition of pragmatism turned out to be "liberal" in the extreme.

Kristol seemed to have a natural propensity for elevating reverence for power over intellectual scruples. In a brilliant essay on Nazism that he published in 1948—Kristol was indeed brilliant, and his pellucid prose style was on a par with Orwell's—he eloquently despaired of the workings of the human mind itself.

After pronouncing rational analysis impotent to explain the Nazi mentality, he concludes about Rudolf Hess that "Hess's psychic processes were not different in kind from those which might be discovered among French barbers, Mid-Western university professors, or composers of letters-from-the-lovelorn in all lands. His unconscious faithfully adhered to the rules of the universal human unconscious, and we see that we are not entirely strangers to the twistings of his mind."

"The rules of the universal human unconscious." The phrase might smack of naive Freudianism, but Kristol seemed never to stop believing that an implacable chaos lay behind the intellect's most rational and ethically sophisticated constructions. As a result, he gave up on principled thinking and became a kind of intellectual *tummler*—the Yiddish term for a mischief-maker, whose power lies in creating prankish distractions. But Kristol had a motive for his *tummling*: the acquisition of power unavailable to intellectuals.

The specter that haunted Jewish intellectuals of Kristol's generation was the *luftmensch*, another Yiddish word meaning, literally, a person who lives in the air: specifically, the intellectual who eats and drinks ideas but who has no real power in the world outside his own mental capacities. Their anxiety was prescient: they would have seen the intellectual's current lack of employment coming from miles away. But Kristol turned the image of the *luftmensch* upside down. He became a cosmopolitan nihilist who enjoyed watching the effects of his ideas on powerful men— Nixon, Reagan—without having any investment in the consequences of his ideas.

When, for example, Kristol mouthed allegiance to New Deal principles and criticized capitalism's soulless aspects, he was executing a Dada performance, playing to his liberal friends as well as playing them like salmon. No intelligent man who advocated the types of radical tax cuts that Kristol did could possibly expect New Deal social welfare commitments to survive intact.

Kristol's much-publicized affection for working-class values and for the Christian Right is in the same vein of toying with ideas without conviction. It was well known that this defender of Christian fundamentalism and Jewish core principles possessed no religious feeling or belief himself. "I've always been a believer," he once said with his usual *tummler*'s facileness. "Don't ask me in what." As for the working class, they had become, for this former Marxist, pure abstraction. If the universal human unconscious ruled existence, what did it matter whether you conceived of a barber as a monster or a saint? The important thing was to use your conceptions as ladders to a level of power that would keep the working class and mugging reality at a good safe distance. After all, this was a man who, in 1988, listed the "public transportation that is a daily trauma" as one of his reasons for leaving New York City.

One of Kristol's most original and memorable essays is one he published about Jewish humor in 1951. It is also his most revealing. At the end of this dazzling reflection, Kristol concludes that:

"Jewish humor dances along a knife-edge that separates religious faith from sheer nihilism." But, he continues, in the modern era, faith in God has become impossible. Thus Jewish humor is dead: "The modern situation, dissolving into murderous nihilism, robs Jewish humor of its victory."

Convinced of the powerlessness of humor and intellect, Kristol spent his life using both as playful vehicles in the pursuit of power. He turned modernity's murderous nihilism into a more comfortable nihilistic game. His most memorable quips are outwardly brilliant but inwardly empty travesties of both humor and intellect: "In the United States today, the law insists that an 18-year-old girl has the right to public fornication in a pornographic movie—but only if she is paid the minimum wage."

The truth is that the issues of wages and free expression could not be further apart, and the question of balancing freedom, decency, and morality could not be less frivolous than Kristol made it out to be in his cute one-liner. His joke is, essentially, nonsense. But it is the kind of profoundly ambitious and disenchanted nonsense that makes a pointed mockery of rational and moral thought. It creates an intellectual and ethical vacuum.

Into this vacuum, enter the Becks, and the Limbaughs, and the Hannitys. Having used seriousness to discredit seriousness, Kristol threw open the door to the pure silliness of luxurious and remunerative antagonism.

"Red Seriousness Versus Blue Seriousness"

Remarkably, since the Civil War the country has been divided into two groups of people, each of whom has an ideal of seriousness that is the radical opposite of the other. On the surface, this conflict doesn't make much sense. Everyone is watching the same TV programs and the same movies; everyone is enjoying the same apps. American culture has been the assimilating fire underneath American society's proverbial melting pot. Politics, however, frames the issues in stark, existential terms. In starkly serious terms. What is the relationship between your money and your government? What is the relationship between your freedom and your government, or between collective freedom and individual freedom? These are among life's most serious questions, and on these questions, the country is divided right down the line.

Here is how two self-contained, absolutely distinct frameworks of seriousness have been created in American politics.

Twenty-five years ago, the Reaganites pronounced government irrelevant, even obstructive, to the improvement of social life. This had the effect of shifting the Republicans' center of operations from politics to culture. In short order, the Reagan revolutionaries invited into their cause the Christian Right, who set their self-contained cultural universe against secular cultural values that the liberals never dreamed would be under explicit siege.

Still, the Christian perspective had to be tempered and made more inclusive. Enter Allan Bloom. In 1987, Bloom published his bestselling *The Closing of the American Mind*, an attack on what he perceived as the coarseness of popular culture and a destructive nihilism masquerading as inclusiveness at the nation's elite universities. Though Bloom was as scathing toward the conservative notion of "values" as he was toward the liberal idea of all values being relative, his disdain for the nihilism and hedonism of contemporary American life was enough to serve conservative political purposes. Neoconservative tricksters like Kristol and Norman Podhoretz immediately put the Christian Right's banner in Bloom's cosmopolitan intellectual's hands and used him, in effect, to marry the religious Right to the mostly secular neoconservatives. They began the work completed by William Bennett in the latter's sensationally popular *The Book of Virtues*.

It should be said that Bloom made it easy for his book to be appropriated by the Right. In it, he gave the impression that it was hopeless to fight for his beloved Great Books, because the Great Books had been driven to extinction by angry left-wing professors and vulgar forms of diversion. High culture was irretrievably lost to the average person. Culture for Bloom now meant not literature or art, but the struggle for the American individual's endangered "soul" (a word repeated throughout his book). This secular Armageddon was vividly embodied by Bloom in his now-notorious image of a solipsistic American teenager masturbating alone in his room while listening to deafening rock and roll. In one stroke, Bloom submerged politics irrevocably, and fertilely, in culture, and he defined culture in the broadest way as the necessity of living a meaningful life. Values, in other words, though he really meant no such thing.

As a result of all this intellectual tumult, one clear distinction stands out among the differences between contemporary liberals and conservatives (the real differences, not the manufactured ones). Liberals think that our politics is broken, because it cannot be a vehicle for the moral renovation of society, while conservatives think our culture is broken, because it cannot be a vehicle for . . . the moral renovation of society.

These conflicting urgencies have given the conservatives mostly the upper hand for over a quarter of a century. Since culture is more immediate to us than the abstract policies and principles of politics—and seemingly more dependable than politics' often fluid expediencies—a politics of culture is going to be more successful than mere politics. For many people, the idea that Republican politics are wholly responsible for the country's ills is hard to accept. You can't feel politics. Rather, such people blame a culture of selfishness and irresponsibility for the deepening malaise (the word that sank President Carter among liberals who thought they smelled a Christian conservative in progressive clothing). You experience selfishness and irresponsibility in the flesh every day.

Let me clarify what the word "culture" means in this context, à la the Christian Right and Bloom's descendants. If hearing the word "culture" makes you think of Rossini, the latest translation of *Anna Karenina*, the Guggenheim Museum, or *The Wire*, then you're probably a liberal—or, at least, an unreconstructed "cosmopolitan" conservative. But if the word "culture" means for you forms of courtship, or sexual preference, or the relationship between parents and children, or the set of rituals that revolve around the ownership and use of a gun, or, most passionately of all, ways of living, and believing, and rejoicing, and suffering, and dying that are hallowed by the religion you practice and embodied in the church you belong to—if, for you, culture does not primarily signify opera or HBO, then you are probably celebrating Sarah Palin's ragged, real-seeming life. In that case, you are what might be called either a heartland or a Bloomian conservative.

Broadly speaking, liberals segregate culture from ordinary existence. They will "do" culture and then "do" the rest of life— gaze at a Vermeer, say, and then work on finding the perfect daycare center. But for conservatives, raising children, using the discipline of faith to endure illness or setback, cherishing life at its conception are cultural tasks and values inseparable from the challenges of everyday living. The liberal idea of culture as edification or diversion implies abundant leisure time. The conservative idea of culture as the practice of getting through life (like the anthropologist's idea of culture) implies time under siege by work and adversity; this is culture defined as the meaningful beliefs and activities that are the response to necessity and adversity. Culture in this sense is as familiar as the eight-hour day, and as intimate as biological function. It is a matter of life and death. Call it visceral, as opposed to fabricated, culture.

This is why Thomas Frank's influential 2004 critique of the Republicans' cultural strategy, *What's the Matter with Kansas?*, has had, despite Obama's victory in 2008, such a negative effect on the Democrats' fortunes, for the simple reason that Frank assured Democrats that they didn't have to respond to the way the Republicans were manipulating visceral culture. Frank cogently argued that the Republicans used cultural issues to distract their constituents from Republican economic policies, which, ironically, were harming the very people who were voting for them. Frank believed that what Democrats had to do to win back the White House was to keep hammering away at Republican-induced economic disparities. For many people, however, faith in visceral culture is intimate and empowering, while faith in politics is like trying to have a conversation with the TV.

Yet visceral culture has its squalid side, too. Visceral culture is often unreflective, which makes it vulnerable to the vicious emotional intensity of racial, religious, and ethnic prejudice. Blindness to the role culture plays in politics, even contempt for raising the subject, also lies behind the Democrats' fatal blindness to the brute fact of race in America. When, during the last Democratic presidential primaries, the Clintons seemed to allude to the subject of Senator Obama's electability in the light of his race, they were accused by many of their fellow Democrats of "playing the race card." It is fairly incredible that it was, for the most part, not until the summer of 2008 that liberals began publicly asking themselves if the country was ready for a black president. That it was not until then that liberals began wondering with any forcefulness whether people really were telling pollsters the truth about their attitudes toward race. ("Will race influence your vote for president?" "Race?! Me? Are you kidding? Of course not!")

It was as though liberals were afraid that if they spoke honestly about racism as a stumbling block to Obama's candidacy, they would be taken for racists themselves. It was as though by ignoring racist attitudes when writing about Senator Obama, liberal commentators conferred on themselves the virtuous idealism that they were fantastically attributing to the country as a whole. It is an elementary psychological fact that we sometimes praise to an absurd degree what makes us slightly uncomfortable—or that we put the source of discomfort in an impossibly ideal light in order to put as much distance as possible between us . . . and the person we fear we may actually be.

Politics, by definition, is the art of making the abstract palpable and real. Within the realm of visceral culture, abstract ideas about life are already embodied in life itself. The Republicans seem to have abandoned Russell Kirk, the intellectual progenitor of modern American conservatism, for Mark Burnett—the creator of *Survivor* and the father of reality television, a form of entertainment in which you come to relish the example of chastised ambition. Reality TV's winners earn your affection by running the gamut of ordeal and humiliation. In the same way, the Republicans have intuitively grasped a new, virulent strain of democracy, accelerated by the Internet, in which authority must be humbled before it is allowed to lead, or to lead again. This framework of seriousness that conservatives have erected around visceral culture is very effective against the liberal framework of seriousness—the belief that inequality and injustice may be defeated by the rational political reorganization of social life. The former seriousness lends itself to stories. The latter seriousness, because it is fundamentally hypothetical, lends itself to theories. As we have seen, a seriousness tied to life retains its freshness longer than one supported only by ideas.

How else to explain Sarah Palin's success? Regardless of who she really is or what she really represents, she is an American story straight out of Oprah's universe. In many ways, Palin is, for her legions of followers, the white Oprah. Like Oprah, she presents the illusion of having made her life her work—the minute she gave up the governorship of Alaska, she turned her very existence into a vocation. Like others who have won the celebrity lottery, she rose to acclaim and sudden wealth, and then was brought savagely low, all the while providing a stream of highly personalized commentary in her Facebook and Twitter postings. But whereas Oprah orchestrates the silly wink behind the facade of seriousness, Palin seems to have silliness coursing through her veins. She has a natural instinct for performing seriousness by humbling herself as a way to re-serious herself.

That inflation-deflation dynamic accounts for the popularity of the reality-television show *Sarah Palin's Alaska*, which happened to be produced in the fall of 2010 by none other than Mark Burnett. America's inflation and then deflation of its public figures is, in fact, an X-ray of American attitudes toward seriousness. We take some public figures so seriously—i.e., they seem like us—that they eventually acquire a gigantic authority and influence. But since no one can lord it too much over anyone else in a democracy—i.e., as they acquire more power and status, they become too much unlike us—that very bigness tips the figure over into silliness. So we cut them down to size, and in their humbling, they become serious—i.e., more like us—once again.

In *Sarah Palin's Alaska*, Palin made a point of humbling herself, again and again: professing fear as she is stuck on a glacier she is attempting to climb; shooting skeet and missing while mistakenly ejecting a shell into her face; being insulted for her "prom hair" by her daughter Bristol; losing to her husband, Todd, in a kayak race. Cleaning fish blood and guts off the bottom of a fishing boat, she mocks herself: "All diva all the time." At one point in this weekly portrayal of her family's summertime expeditions, she exclaims, "I was so cocky, I'm being punished for it."

At around the same time that Palin was re-seriousing herself, Obama made a point of appearing at a White House window, for all the world's photographers to see, holding an ice pack to his mouth after a stray elbow during a basketball game put a cut in his lip that required twelve stitches. The stitches were not in time. Obama was learning, stiffly, to play the humbling game too late. It was Palin's humiliation by the liberal media that made her a heroine in the eyes of her supporters in the first place. Then came her books, and her gig at Fox News, and her own media triumph over the media. With her new show, she was humbling herself once more. You realized yet again that although Palin, with the help of economic meltdown, may have lost McCain the election, she and her admirers won the political war.

The remarkable thing about *Sarah Palin's Alaska* was that even as you recoiled from her smarmy asides about the importance of family, repeated with mechanical coldness many times each episode, you found yourself moved by some of the most deliberately scripted, patently insincere scenes in the history of modern entertainment. Even as you were repelled by her silliness, you were seduced by her rendition of seriousness.

The entire staff of the *New York Review of Books* could not but melt when Todd picks up their son Trig, who has Down syndrome, and the child laughs that self-devouring, self-delighted laugh of little boys as his father carries him into the house. There is nothing more humbling than a son or daughter hurt by nature beyond love's repair. Several times, Palin uses the wilderness backdrop to make the point that "Mother Nature" always wins. In that regard, the entire series is devoted to illustrating survivalist profiles in courage. The Palins zip around in small death traps as Sarah reminds us that Alaska "leads the country in [small-plane] fatalities." Still, they must fly. Ferocious-seeming brown bears approach their canoe. Still, they must fish. We are told that climbers routinely fall into crevasses that are several hundred feet deep. Still, they must ascend.

This, we are meant to see, is how people live with dignity without the indignity of government intrusion. This is how people get through their lives. And this, indeed, is what blue-state seriousness does not understand about its invisible bonds with red-state seriousness. We are all borne hither and thither by the tides of work and love. Todd struggles with their eldest son, Track. Sarah struggles with their eldest daughter, Bristol. "Don't retreat, just reload!" she exhorts Bristol, who at that very moment, on a different channel, was magnifying her mother's humility by being humbled herself, yet "reloading" herself, week after week, on *Dancing with the Stars.* An episode entirely devoted to the Palins fishing for halibut on a commercial fishing boat showed Sarah (ever so daintily) thwacking a fish unconscious with a club and then gutting another one. "It smells like work. It smells like money," she declares. Liberals get their Omega-3 amiably, as a supplement, and that is the problem, all those federal supplements and entitlements. But liberals cannot talk about creating jobs unless they know the true facts of work. Even the Palin children are named after facts, as if they were eponymous figures of myth symbolizing the unyielding, untranscendent nature of life: Bristol (after Alaska's Bristol Bay); Track; Willow; Piper (after Todd's airplane). Liberals, on the other hand, are weak with transcendent, idealistic talk.

And liberals still don't get the Palin appeal, especially liberal women, perhaps because she is the hardworking female professional's worst nightmare: the cunning amoral sylph who uses her sexual appeal to get what she doesn't deserve. In *The New Yorker*, Nancy Franklin watched *Sarah Palin's Alaska* and threw up her hands: "I can't say what Palin is really up to with this show." The only response the *New York Times'* Alessandra Stanley had to Palin's masterstroke of self-humbling as she clutched the glacier in terror was to sneer that Palin's "high-pitched voice is so piercing it could trigger an avalanche."

The most mind-boggling misperception of Palin's appeal came just as her new show premiered, from *New York Times* columnist Maureen Dowd. Comparing Palin to Marilyn Monroe, Dowd proclaimed that Marilyn was superior to Sarah because the former had read "some" literature and had a big library, while the unlettered latter couldn't speak English well. "In Marilyn's America, there were aspirations," lamented Dowd, who apparently had forgotten the name "Doris Day." But Marilyn was also used, abused, and humiliated by men all her life. Sarah won't allow anyone to get over on her, and she gets her own back every time. Women are drawn to her precisely because she is the anti-Marilyn.

Palin might well run for president, but she would never win. She is too thin-skinned, self-centered, ill-informed, and mean-spirited. Despite her storytelling and image-making capacities, she cannot hide the earthy, homely, everyday fact that her own social type in the grand human narrative is that of The Bitch. At one point in her show, a fisherman puts the still-beating heart of a halibut in her hand. It is a strange, wondrous, unsettling thing. Palin looks at it for an instant and then tosses it indifferently overboard. "Too weird," she says. Her own heart is that of a shallow teenage girl. She is Paris Hilton with sled dogs. Her political destiny is to be a sometimes consequential political outlier.

But a political figure with Sarah Palin's mythmaking talents and common touch, yet without her deficiencies, a political figure that had her seriousness about the way people live their lives without her silliness about the way she has turned her own life into a stage for image creation . . . that would be a whole different story.

Parties of Rage and Incredulity

The two absolutely distinct frameworks of seriousness are the creation of a fatal political dynamic that enables extremist personalities like Palin to thrive. The more serious the issues are, the more they become delivered up to an adversarial momentum that reduces them to a silliness in which absolute antagonism becomes a reassuring norm.

This is why half the country is enraged, and the other half is incredulous. The party of rage shouts, "I'm mad as hell, and I'm not going to take this anymore!" The party of incredulity cries, "I'm shocked as hell, and I'm not going to listen to this anymore!"

Each side follows the other's grievances and recriminations with pornographic intensity, to the point that the political landscape is defined not by ungratifying facts but by titillating incidents.

At this point, a peculiar development occurs. The more the party of incredulity is convinced of the immovable wrongheadedness of the party of rage, the happier it gets about its own moral position. The sound of rational protest underneath the Right's robotic blustering goes blissfully unheard. The fundamental flaw of the liberal mind has always been a ravenous hunger for a moral superiority that will serve as the permanent last word of any argument. In that sense, the new radical Right is a godsend to the needy liberal conscience. And the deeply gratified moral indignation of the liberals, which has a paralyzing effect on liberal politics, is a godsend to the frenzies of the new radical Right.

Like a kinetic desktop gadget, the battle between America's two political seriousnesses has its own self-perpetuating dynamic.

The Right reveres authority and scorns government. The Left admires government and disdains authority. People on the Right draw strength from the feeling that they are being marginalized by the powers that be: "elected" products of impermeable elite networks. People on the Left draw strength from the feeling that they are being victimized by the powers-that-shouldn't-be: shadowy billionaires and secret campaign donors. The Right does not want to admit that without mountains of money, no one in this country can influence the political system. But the Left does not want to admit that beyond a certain saturation point of super-wealth, as in all plutocracies, money has to bow to other factors. See Ross Perot and Steve Forbes. See Michael Bloomberg's unimpressive national prospects. The fact is that both sides are swimming in appalling amounts of dough.

The Right seeks elected positions while vowing to obliterate government. The Left speaks of moral obligation while deriding anyone's claim to embody it. The Right accuses cultural "elites" of clubby exclusivity while throwing its support behind clubbily exclusive business elites. The Left complains about the Right's clandestine donors and locustlike lobbyists while welcoming its own clandestine donors and locustlike lobbyists. The Left looks to government for salvation yet thinks itself above the dirty expediencies of politics. The Right looks for salvation to the dirty expediencies of politics yet condemns the operations of government. Neither side will recognize that it is neck-deep in the contradictions and hypocrisies practiced by the other side.

As a result, neither side can see the kernel of sense at the heart of the other side's efforts to prevail. In 2010, liberals were scratching their heads over just why Virginia Thomas, Justice Clarence Thomas's wife, would leave a message on Anita Hill's answering machine asking her to apologize for accusing Thomas of sexual harassment all those many years ago. For them, the (titillating) incident crystallizes their current state of incredulity. They consider it incredible that Ms. Thomas is still so blinded by anger that she fails to see the obvious, which is that Hill was telling the truth while Thomas was lying and that he was clearly unfit, on the basis of Hill's testimony about his character, to sit on the Supreme Court.

Let us leave aside what is without doubt the truly fascinating question of Thomas's character, as well as the fact that though no one ever demonstrated before Congress or a court of law that Thomas was lying when he said he had not rented pornographic videos, the evidence later proved that he was. Perhaps retaliating for the way Gary Hart was felled by the blunt weapon of his private life, Hill and her enablers made a fateful mistake. Once the Pandora's box of unquantifiable private behavior was opened even wider, and deployed as a public standard, American politics was irrevocably degraded.

On the eve of the midterm elections and what proved to be the most triumphant moment for a broad-based right-wing movement since Reagan, Virginia Thomas experienced a crystallization of her rage. She wanted to tell Hill that what comes around, goes around. She wanted to crow that the rage in the form of liberal fury that almost toppled her black husband as conservatives watched, unbelieving, was now about to cripple Hill's black president, in the form of conservative fury, as liberals watched, unbelieving. About the fluidity of American rage and incredulity, she was onto something. But don't expect anyone who believes Ms. Thomas's side is seriously wrong ever to concede that she might also be seriously right. That would mean acknowledging that one of the biggest obstacles to seriousness in American politics is the blind complicity of political adversaries in each other's momentum. It would mean acknowledging that buried deep in each side's grievances is a shared discontent.

Whose Counterculture Is It?

We've heard for years how the subversive culture of the 1960s was gradually assimilated by the fevered commercial culture of the

1980s and 1990s. Free love, drugs, "do your own thing," public obscenity, provocative dress—what once shocked the American middle class is now the stuff of everyday American experience. Viagra, you might say, is Woodstock in pills.

Yet although society may have changed, politics remained the same. As the go-go imperatives of commercial life seemed to make just about every solid social norm melt into air, politicians went about their routine business. They cut or raised taxes, balanced the budget or ran a deficit, made war or preserved the peace. Through it all, they kept their hands off any legislative engine that would have a radically transformative effect on everyday life.

Predictable, routine, unchanging government became something like a sanctuary from the *Animal House* atmosphere of much American social and cultural life. The halls of power seemed a refuge for all those who had been terrified of the counterculture in the 1960s, and felt alienated by the commercial assimilation of countercultural values post-1960s. Patriotism, religion, morality—in the form of Christian-tinted government that promised stability amid all the social and cultural daily upheaval—became the war cry against the destabilizing culture of gratification.

But nowadays, government itself seems dynamic and full of change. It promises to sweep away the familiar contours of everyday experience. The mainstream assimilation of countercultural values is no longer just a social phenomenon. Government seems to have become countercultural, too. A black man is in the White House. A transformation is taking place in the relationship between our health and the public realm (Our Bodies, Our Politicians). Some type of restructuring of the government's relationship to American business is occurring.

In society, culture, and now politics, what was once considered countercultural is today the establishment. Thus it's no surprise that what was once considered the establishment—the war cry of patriotism, religion, and morality—is the new counterculture. Tea Party calls for reducing the deficit are as extreme as any New Left indictment of the government's role in social life. The parallels between today's right-wing radicals and the radical tactics of the 1960s are striking. Consider the relationship between the Tea Partiers and the Beats, who were the essence of the 1950s and early 1960s counterculture, and who were led by those two icons of countercultural seriousness, Allen Ginsberg and Jack Kerouac.

Like the Beats, the Tea Partiers are driven by that maddeningly contradictory principle, subject to countless interpretations, at the heart of all American protest movements: individual freedom. The shared DNA of American dissent might be one answer to the question of why the Tea Partiers, so anachronistic in their opposition to any type of government, exert such an astounding appeal.

Of course, on the surface, the differences between "Beat" and "Tea Party" are so immense as to make comparisons seem frivolous. The Beats, though pacifist, were essentially apolitical. Kerouac's hatred of the Left at the end of his life seemed most of all to be a revulsion against the New Left's enthusiastic hating. The Beats' aims were spiritual and sexual liberation, and a unifying wholeness with nature. Insofar as they had sociopolitical ambitions, their goals—abolishing censorship, protecting the environment, opposing what Ginsberg called "the military-industrial machine civilization"—were the stuff of poetry, not organized politics. In contrast, the Tea Partiers seek the political objectives of "individual liberty, limited government and economic freedom." Balancing the budget and rejecting cap-and-trade are their hearts' desires, not sexual revolution or the quest for spiritual harmony through the use of Zen meditation and hallucinogenics.

Still, American dissent turns on a tradition of troublemaking, suspicion of elites, and feelings of powerlessness, no matter where on the political spectrum dissent takes place. Surely just about every Tea Partier agrees with Ginsberg on the enervating effect of the liberal media. Recall from an earlier chapter his arch-sincere question to America: "Are you going to let our emotional life be run by Time Magazine?"

More seriously, the origin of the word "beat" has a connection to the Tea Partiers' sense that they are being marginalized as the country is taken away from them. According to Ginsberg, to be "beat" most basically signified "exhausted, at the bottom of the world, looking up or out . . . rejected by society." Barack Obama meant much the same thing when, during the presidential primaries, he notoriously said that "in a lot of these communities in big industrial states like Ohio and Pennsylvania, people have been beaten down so long, and they feel so betrayed by government." That he went on to characterize such people as "bitter" souls who "cling to their guns or religion or antipathy toward people who aren't like them" only strengthened the anxiety among proto–Tea Partiers that they were about to be "rejected by society." That they were about to be consigned to the dustbin of history along with Nixon's "silent majority."

When the Tea Party came along, however, the silent majority started to get its voice back. Liberals could well be drawn nostalgically to the Beats nowadays, because all the countercultural energy belongs to the other side. "When will you be worthy of your million Trotskyites?" Ginsberg asked his fellow Americans in his poem "America." The Tea Party has an answer to that rhetorical question. A former community organizer might be in the White House, but the Tea Partiers taking to the streets are now the ones supposedly influenced by Saul Alinsky's Trotskyish *Rules for Radicals*, not the liberals who watch horrified and silent from the sidelines.

Then again, the Beats were as much at odds with the liberals of their time as the Tea Partiers are with the liberals of today. The same liberal air of elite-seeming abstraction that provokes the Tea Partiers drove the Beats around the bend. For the Beats, liberals were part of the power structure: they spoke loftily about conscience and social obligation yet lived comfortably within the plush boundaries of universities, law firms, and financial institutions. Worst of all, liberals accepted the government's role in organizing their lives. In the secret file the FBI kept on him, Ginsberg was described by J. Edgar Hoover himself as having a dangerous "antipathy" toward government. Against the liberals' seeming complicity with the status quo, the Beats took to the road in quest of what Jack Kerouac (quoting Oswald Spengler) called a "second religiousness" within Western civilization. With their noisy commitment to their churches, the Tea Partiers also seem to want their religious communities to take the place of government in their lives. They would certainly sympathize with Ginsberg's antipathy.

Perhaps this mutual feeling of cultural exile is why some Tea Partiers share with the Beats a reverence for the power of imprecation—in the matter of unbridled speech, they would have been on the side of the verbally unrestrained Ginsberg. True, the Tea Partiers' unnerving habit of bringing guns to town hall meetings would have repelled the Beats. But another Beat guru, the novelist William S. Burroughs, fetishized guns, accidentally killing his wife while trying to shoot a glass off her head. Violence, implicit or explicit, comes with the "beaten" state of mind. So does theatricality, since playing roles—and manipulating symbols—is often the first resort of people who do not feel acknowledged for being who they really are. Ginsberg didn't merely write poetry, and he didn't simply recite it. He turned his poetry readings into theatrical performances of Dionysian proportions. Some people might say the difference between Allen Ginsberg and Glenn Beck is the difference between psychedelic and psychopathic, but Beck might well envy Ginsberg's attempt, in 1967, to help Abbie Hoffman and a band of antiwar protesters levitate the Pentagon by means of tantric chanting, though Beck would no doubt concentrate his telepathic efforts on the IRS.

American seriousness about freedom is a many-splendored thing, and multifaceted, too. "We drove in his old Chevy," Kerouac says, with portentous joy, in *On the Road*. In the course of the manic tirade that gave birth to the Tea Party, Rick Santelli of CNBC referred to the 1954 Chevy, "maybe the last great car to come out of Detroit." In that shared love for a profoundly symbolic American experience, you can detect the beginnings of a beautiful friendship. For politics used to make, as the saying went, strange bedfellows. Not anymore. Now it makes for estranged bedfellows, who hate each other all the more when they realize, in horror, that their different worldviews are often shaped by similar impulses.

Comedy Central Seriously Reconsidered

Even the comedians' newfound seriousness does not seem to have saved them from being swept along by the same attitudes that drive their satirical targets. During the Cold War, the United States and the Soviet Union carried on their conflict through so-called proxy wars all over the world. In much the same way, our politics has created two proxies of seriousness that are now battling it out in some media-ized circus arena: Fanaticism and Sarcasm. And they both are complicit with each other. There is not just the furtive embrace between Tea Party and Beats. There is the furtive embrace between Tea Party laughter and Comedy Central laughter.

Invented by Jon Stewart and fine-tuned by Stephen Colbert, Comedy Central laughter attains its ideal form when it encounters a figure representing authority or expertise. The premise of both comedians' shows is that such figures are responsible for most of the world's folly. The worst authority figures are the politicians, who, by definition, are stupid and venal in proportion to the amount of power they possess. Right behind them are the experts, who are almost always the authors of books, and whose theories about life woefully pale when playfully pushed. Confronted by such asses, who are pompous enough to expect other people to abide by their ideas, Stewart and Colbert mock, taunt, outrage, and ironize until the expert or authoritative guest liquefies like metal in a forge. Of course, liberal guests get a kind of complicit wink at the end of their ordeal, but only after they've been de-expertized and un-authoritied and returned to the common mass of couch-dwelling humanity.

They are returned, in other words, to the couch alongside those Tea Party figures who publicly excoriate the United Nations, the Department of Education, any type of tax legislation, and the entire collection of experts and authority figures who, together, make up what is known as modern-day "government." For all the radical differences between them, both the comedians and the Tea Partiers spring from democracy's latent pathology, which is the belief that in the name of democracy, expertise and authority must not be allowed to serve as social levers elevating certain individuals over others.

The Tea Party pratfalls that provoke liberals to laugh incite the Tea Partiers to laugh, too. Sarah Palin's wink, Donald Trump's histrionic sincerity, the deliberate earnestness displayed by some Tea Party legislators about the most far-fetched views—it is all meant to be Comedy Right-of-Central. These people are upending the sacred cows of established fact, of intellectual expertise, of elected authority. They are doing all this to very different ends than Stewart and Colbert, obviously. But they are drawing their energy from the hyper-democratic hatred of expertise and authority. Just like Stewart and Colbert.

Yet once you begin railing against what you consider the wrong type of authority and expertise, what do you do when the wind begins to blow in the opposite direction? Nearly a hundred years ago in Germany, a similar situation prevailed. After the vast devastation of the First World War and the official lies that led hundreds of thousands of men to their deaths, the forefathers of Comedy Central, the Dadaists, also made it their job to see through the claims of authority and expertise. They wrote and recited nonsense poetry because they believed that nonsense was a liberation from fake public meaning. They made photomontages—mash-ups—showing German statesmen bathing nude, implying that underneath the pomp and ceremony of official power lay an amoral puniness, symbolized by these bare, unlovely bodies. The Dadaists embodied a general rage against hypocrisy. But they also helped accelerate the general madness. Their principled rage created an atmosphere where all kinds of rage were possible.

You have to wonder what the fate of serious public life will be as Fanaticism and Sarcasm continue to battle it out.

A Fine Mess: Red-State Elitism Versus Blue-State Elitism

The paralyzing loggerheads at which the two sides find themselves occasionally needs a side debate. As soon as extremism and fanaticism show their silly faces, they reach for a concept that might make them appear serious. "Elitism" is always on hand for that purpose.

"Elitism" is a grave accusation in our democracy. It connotes the ultimate antidemocratic personality. If you are an elite, then the perception is that you got what you have through connections, not merit. You are considered to be blind and indifferent to the lives of your fellow citizens. The general, democratic belief is that the bubble of privilege that elites live in allows them to act for themselves without taking anyone else into account.

Needless to say, both Right and Left have absolutely distinct, and absolutely serious ideas of what it means to be an "elite." In both cases, the original meaning of the term has been lost.

"Elitism" as modern political curse in America originated with Senator Joseph McCarthy, who used it to refer to American Communists and fellow travelers. Since you had to read up on Communism to become a Communist—unlike becoming a Democrat or a Republican—McCarthy's definition of elitism was synonymous with intellectualism, by which he meant a sympathy for Communism. When people on the Right throw around the word "elitist," they are, like the authors of the "Contract from America," engaged in an act of nostalgia.

Today's anti-elitists are also blind to the true sociopolitical meaning of the word. In the classic definition of modern elites, constructed by three sociologists of the early twentieth century— Vilfredo Pareto, Gaetano Mosca, and Robert Michels—elites were those who possessed consequential power. They were the wealthy businessmen, the politicians, the generals. A stratum of efficacious figures is also what C. Wright Mills meant by the "power elite" in his influential 1956 book of the same name. The Tea Party notion that elites are characterized by a certain type of cultural pedigree would have made the original theorists chuckle.

In fact, the Tea Party's identification of elites with cultural rather than political qualities is a Marxist idea. It was formulated by the Italian socialist Antonio Gramsci, a rough contemporary of Pareto, Mosca, and Michels. Gramsci believed that the people who make the culture, from journalists to playwrights, shape popular consciousness. Change the way culture represents the world, and you change the political system. (Mills Americanized Gramsci's notion when, in 1960, he called for a "new left" counterculture to combat the power elite.) When Sarah Palin, Rush Limbaugh, Michele Bachmann, Newt Gingrich, and the rest perform their rage against the liberal elite, they are attacking products of supposedly Ivy League schools, who exert their influence by directing the culture. Yet when they declaim on the sanctity of family and church, they are following Gramsci's counsel. They themselves are attempting to manipulate popular values just like the cultural elites they claim to despise.

It was a Catholic conservative, Michael Novak, who published an essay in 1989 called "The Gramscists Are Coming," advising the right wing to adopt Gramscist tactics to influence customs and conventions. He was reformulating culture as what we have called visceral culture: the means by which people get through their daily lives—the way they raise their children, understand good and evil, define the moment when life begins. Novak was, to recall our definition of visceral culture, defining culture anthropologically, not intellectually. The result was Patrick Buchanan's astringent declaration at the 1992 Republican convention: "There is a religious war going on in our country for the soul of America. It is a cultural war, as critical to the kind of nation we will one day be as was the Cold War itself." Thus, while the New Left, inspired by Gramsci, made its "long march through the institutions" and haplessly proceeded to take over English departments in an attempt to reshape consciousness, Buchanan and President Reagan's New Right, also inspired by Gramsci, made its more effective long march through the media in an effort to do the same. This could be why, currently, the Right has Fox while the Left has Comedy Central. Both Right and Left, however, define "elite" in cultural terms.

Yet, although liberals may be quick to point out the irony of the Tea Party being funded by the real elites—the ones with the most money—they don't like using the word "elite" to describe these rich bêtes noires. Liberals might titter and scoff at Palin's taunts of "elitist," but they secretly cherish the idea of being the true American elites. They would rather die than call a wealthy businessman a member of the "elite." This is because, for liberals, elitism means being above crass material considerations. That is why conservatives hate them.

In his seminal 1941 book *The Managerial Revolution*, James Burnham observed that society was becoming divided into two classes: the people who owned the corporations, and the people who ran them. To simplify Burnham's ideas, the former were concerned with making money, the latter with ideas about how to spend it. Buchanan was taking a page out of Burnham when he declared that "America's great middle class has got to start standing up to the environmental extremists who put insects, rats, and birds ahead of families, workers, and jobs." He was claiming that the industrious producers of wealth—which somehow had come to include non-energetic shareholders—had to stand up to the parasitical class of overeducated slackers who use wealth to pursue goals that add nothing to the nation's economic well-being.

This kind of outrageous illogic drives liberals up a wall. How can liberals be above material considerations, they ask themselves. It is liberals who want to strengthen the social safety net and want government to shore up small businesses with tax breaks and loans. It is liberals who want to improve everyone's material life for the sake of equality and justice.

But there is the liberals' problem. Even when they speak of improving material life, liberals are touting nonmaterial premises that lead to the nonmaterial goals of equality and justice. Conservatives talk concretely about lowering taxes to stimulate economic growth. Liberals talk abstractly about raising taxes to create an ideal. In this way, the dispute between conservatism and liberalism comes down to, in a mutation of Burnham's formulation, materialists versus nonmaterialists. Or, to put the conflict in Novak's and Buchanan's terms: people who struggle materially and are burdened by the facts of life versus people who take their material comforts for granted and think in abstract, ameliorative terms. Ordinary joes versus elitists.

Deluded as it may sound to liberal ears, there is a psychological truth to this conservative aversion to idea-driven elites that gives their aversion its sticking power. In the end, it does not matter that liberal policies are driven by considerations of justice, while conservative policies are driven by considerations of wealth. Liberals are the party of ideas, and ideas have a certain entropic property. They flatter their originators. Being the proud possessor of a noble idea of change often makes it easier to accept things as they are.

This moral vanity of the liberal intellectual is what Peter

Viereck was referring to in "The Revolt Against the Elite," his 1955 essay exploring the forces that sustained McCarthyism. Viereck pointed to the "almost infinite smugness" of the liberal who "is forever making quite unnecessary sacrifices of principle to expediency." Both liberals and conservatives might recognize, for their own reasons, naturally, what Viereck means. When President Obama puts tens of millions more people on Medicaid without the courage to legislate federal subsidies for it, thus making the change at the expense of the middle class, whose insurance premiums are now soaring—when such self-canceling policies rear their smiling faces, liberalism is proclaiming morally superior ideas without jeopardizing its status by acting on them.

Michels had a name for this entropic nature of organized good intentions. He called it "the iron law of oligarchy." His law states that the power of every social group, no matter where it is situated on the political spectrum, will finally come to rest in the hands of a small number of individuals. More generally, Michels believed that every social group concerns itself most of all with preserving and maintaining its power. For Michels, conservation of power and status was the essential activity of any elite. So when Tea Partiers rail against the liberals' complacent theorizing and high-flown insularity, they are inadvertently deploring the very qualities that keep liberalism toothless and ineffectual. What these conservatives hate about liberalism is really the inherent conservatism of liberal elites.

Two brands of anti-elitism. Two types of unwitting elitism. Two serious frameworks for both. And the twain shall never meet.

Finale

Career Versus Calling

From the public arenas of culture and politics, let us return to where we began—to the realms of private experience and personal destiny.

Seriousness is not some elevated state of mind that exists outside experience. It does not depend on skill or intelligence. As we have said, it is organic. We inherit the capacity to be serious when we are given the gift of life and then find work through which we may fully live.

Career versus calling. It's an old distinction, one that you almost never hear anymore. But it has everything to do with the context of seriousness in contemporary life.

When I was just out of graduate school, I thought that I might like to work in book publishing. Looking through the newspapers' "Help Wanted" ads, I found an opening at a publisher called Dover Books. Its specialty was reprinting classic works of literature in inexpensive paperback editions. Dover produced, for example, an elegantly designed pocket-size edition of William Blake's *Songs of Innocence and Experience*, and the out-of-print autobiography of Lorenzo Da Ponte, Mozart's librettist and the first professor of Italian at Columbia University. I had cherished these books from the time I was a boy. I was so devoted to reading them in Dover's exquisite editions that you might even say I had attended Dover University. I applied for the job and was invited to come in for an interview.

When I arrived at Dover's offices, I was ready to jump at the chance to take the job if it was offered to me. After a mild, even gentle interrogation, the elderly woman who had conducted the interview told me that the job was mine if I wanted it. I'll never forget what she said next. "A lot of people have had very nice careers here," she told me.

In other words, I could have—to use an old expression—"made a life" at Dover if I had wanted to. It would not have been merely a job. A job you do strictly for money. As you perform it, you hold your essential self—your passions and dreams—at a remove from the work you are engaged in. Who you are when you are at your job and who you are when you are not at your job are two entirely separate people.

A career is different. A career invites you to align who you are with what you work at. It is half a calling. Even when a lawyer is "off" from work, he or she has the type of temperament that enjoys solving intellectual puzzles. A doctor is still fascinated by the workings of the human body; she is still inspired by the thought of saving a life when she is away from her office or the hospital. A career requires just enough of you when you are away from it to keep you inside it for the duration of your working life.

Short of money, worried about the future, excited by the idea that I would be working with literature, my life's great passion, I heard the word "career" and something inside me took a leap. I almost said yes to a career at Dover Books. But I never took the job. Instead, I went back to graduate school. A career had boundaries of time and space, and my love of literature had no boundaries: it spilled over into every minute of my existence. Even as I slept, my molecules were relishing some passage from Montaigne.

I came to understand that the difference between a career and a calling was that you are compelled to pursue the latter even when you are not being compensated for it. You have to pay for education and training to have a career. Once you embark on one, you need to be paid in order to make having a career worthwhile. That is why a career requires institutional guidance and even apprenticeship. That is why a career must have an office or institution in which to practice it. You might even say that a job places you in a preexisting office, while a career opens a new one. You can pursue a calling, on the other hand, in the middle of the night while you are in the middle of a field. With a calling, you fulfill your destiny in your work. Your destiny is to live seriously. You can do that anywhere, so long as you are free.

The work of a calling draws from your life itself. Poets were once said to be called by their muse. Clerics are called by God. Both figures turn their life into their work.

Lawyers, doctors, architects, et al., have a life half in their work, half outside it. The pleasure they take in the intellectual challenges of their work is deeply rooted in their characters and temperaments. But while the man or woman who pursues a calling turns every experience into his or her work, the "professional" has to leave her life at the door when she goes into the office, into her practice. There is no place for her most intimate feelings, fears, and obsessions in her work. The tradesman has even less use for his life in what he does for a living.

Yet a lawyer, doctor, architect, carpenter, electrician, or landscaper may turn his or her career into a calling. The artist or cleric may descend into silliness.

Consider the novelist who is writing to attract attention and make a splash. Compare him to a carpenter who takes for granted the fact that he works for money. The need to tailor his work to his "target audience" will leech away the novelist's attention. The purpose of fulfilling his destiny in his work will give way to the more shallow motivation of pandering to what he calculates is the taste of other people. Even continuity will be lost to him: the big book means more to him than the patient body of work.

The carpenter, on the other hand, has long ago assimilated the fact that he took up his trade to make a living and not to express himself. For that very reason, he is free to express himself. The challenge of making or repairing something holds his absolute attention. The vision of a perfectly made thing imbues him with a sense of purpose. Even continuity belongs to him: the thing that he is creating or fixing will be part of a body of work that will ensure his reputation and the continuance of more work. He is in thrall to his craft, to what he is making. That is how a job becomes a calling.

The lawyer, doctor, and architect make their careers wholly a calling when they pursue their work beyond the institutional or official framework of remuneration and status. Their work is transformed into a calling when, in the utter intensity of attention, purpose, and continuity, the lawyer loses himself in the human immediacy of a trial, the surgeon surrenders himself to the urgent process of repairing a life, the architect becomes diffused into the details of her creation. Just as Picasso said that his hand was guided by what he was painting, these people are called by a power deep within them that responds to something outside their egos' immediate needs. That is how a career becomes a calling. It happens in an instant.

The fact is that we judge seriousness in work by the degree to which work possesses the quality of a calling. How sincere and self-surrendering is a person at his work? To what extent are attention, purpose, and continuity present? The interesting twist is that attention, purpose, and continuity can animate work that is not, on the surface, a calling at all. They can also be entirely absent from paths of life that are considered high callings.

Attention. Purpose. Continuity. First, they need to be called. The question is what calls them.

Seriousness as a Form of Heroism

Remember Matthew Arnold? He defined "high seriousness" exclusively in the realm of culture. For him, high seriousness meant poetry that expressed a "criticism of life." When I started this book, I believed that Arnold had not been able to connect his notion of criticism of life to ordinary life itself. Then I went back and thought some more about the line of poetry that he chose to exemplify his idea. Arnold took it from the great medieval poet Dante's masterpiece, *The Divine Comedy*. The line occurs in that epic poem's last part, called *Paradiso*:

In la sua volontade e nostra pace

In His will is our peace

Thinking about Arnold for a while now, I am beginning to see what the old boy meant.

Arnold was raised as a Christian, but he saw the crumbling of religious faith all around him. He had a dark view of life without God. In "Dover Beach," his most famous poem, he wrote that:

. . . the world, which seems
To lie before us like a land of dreams,
So various, so beautiful, so new,
Hath really neither joy, nor love, nor light,
Nor certitude, nor peace, nor help for pain;
And we are here as on a darkling plain
Swept with confused alarms of struggle and flight,
Where ignorant armies clash by night.

Arnold the moralist believed that "high seriousness" would be an adequate substitute for faith in such a stormy world. But the moralist held poetry to be the highest high seriousness. And for Arnold the working poet, the only response to a confusing, godless world, without faith and without any absolute authority to keep people protected and safe, was love for another human being.

Just before the despairing description of the world from "Dover Beach" that I've quoted above, Arnold wrote this line: "Ah, love, let us be true / To one another!" Arnold deliberately never tells us to whom he is declaring himself. He seems, in fact, not to be addressing anyone at all. Instead he is proclaiming a principle of existence, one that would create a realm of light opposed to the arena of darkness he has just portrayed.

His plea for love and trust is Arnold's secular version of "In His will is our peace." Without God, we find our peace in those bonds with other people that we forge with love. But our attachment to others does not stop with the people we know. At their furthest point of contact, our bonds to other people are formed or severed, every minute of every day, in the work we do in the world. All work has a usefulness to human life. The more profoundly we lose ourselves in our work, the more profoundly our work affects other people. Care for our work is care for others.

If that sounds—to some people—too spiritual to be taken seriously, allow me to give you a worldly example of what I mean about a calling rising up out of work in the spirit of love.

Chesley "Sully" Sullenberger, the commercial pilot who crashlanded US Airways Flight 1549 in the Hudson River in 2009, after a flock of birds disabled one of its engines, was immediately hailed as a "hero." But he did not act heroically. He acted seriously. Responsible for the lives of 155 passengers and his crew, Sullenberger did not crack under the strain of a life-and-death situation. He guided the Airbus 320 onto the freezing river expertly and coolly, and waited until his crew evacuated all the passengers and then left the plane themselves before he abandoned his post. He acted responsibly, professionally, skillfully, morally.

He acted like a commercial airline pilot.

He did what just about any commercial airline pilot would have done in a similar situation. Like Sullenberger, all such pilots are highly trained and experienced fliers, with hundreds of hours of flying time before signing on with a commercial carrier, usually including many hours as fighter pilots in the U.S. Air Force. Like him, they are cool under pressure, responsible, skillful, moral—in their professional setting—human beings.

Or, to put it yet another way, Sullenberger did something that seems to be increasingly rare in American life. He did his job. He didn't shirk his duties, cut corners, make excuses, blame someone else, or fail the people—his clients, you might say—who put their trust in him in a commercial context. He didn't lie, steal, defraud, embezzle, or claim to be one type of person when he was actually someone entirely different.

He focused his attention, persisted in his purpose, and carried through to the end. Again, he was not heroic. He was serious.

But perhaps because we have grown so used to hearing about investors who pilfer rather than invest; legislators who bribe, buy, and sell instead of legislate; respected journalists who pander to power instead of tell the truth; politicians who trim their sails instead of serve their constituents—perhaps because we are so weary of people who seem to be playing roles instead of fulfilling responsibilities, we regard anyone who does what he is paid to do, or who is what he claims to be, as a hero.

What, after all, were Sullenberger's alternatives when he discovered that his plane was about to go down? To hand over the controls to his copilot and run screaming through the cabin? To sit there drinking scotch and popping Xanax and praying that everything would be okay? To parachute out and leave passengers and crew to their fate? (In fact, commercial planes don't carry parachutes. That's why hijackers looking for an airborne getaway always have to ask for them.) Sullenberger's only choice was to land the plane in order to save himself and everyone on board.

Of course, seen in this perspective, Sullenberger's breathtaking grace under pressure does not fit the definition of heroism. When we hear the word "hero," we think of people who do have a choice in life-and-death situations. The firefighter who runs into the burning building to rescue someone has a choice to do so or not. Sacrificing his life for another person's is not part of the job description. Surely there are times when other considerations—like his children, or other people who depend on him for their survival—hold a firefighter back from rushing into a situation where he might have to give his life to save someone else's. No one would accuse him of cowardice, but that choice to risk his life for another is what makes him a hero. The same goes for the person who jumps into a frozen river to save someone who is drowning, or the person who jumps into the path of a speeding car to sweep a child to safety. They all have a choice. Sullenberger didn't. He acted exemplarily, admirably, beautifully. But he did not act heroically. He was, he said, "just doing my job." Socrates, too, our avatar of seriousness, was "just doing his job." A philosopher lives and dies by the truth. Socrates lived and died by the truth. Therefore, Socrates was just doing his job as a philosopher.

In a world "swept with confused alarms of struggle and flight," as Arnold wrote, Sullenberger submerged his will in his work. *In la sua volontade e nostra pace.* And his work was to save the people in his care. The job that Sullenberger had to do was another name for love.

If we could, in absolute attention, see that the purpose of life is to create the conditions for more life; if we could see that every moment of existence lies on a continuum of moments stretching back into the past and forward into the future—then we would realize that, from naked minute to naked minute, we are guiding our interconnected relationships toward as safe a landing as possible on what amounts to a fragile sheet of water.

If we were able to be aware, as Sullenberger suddenly was, of the world summoning us in this way through our work, then just doing our job would become the most meaningful act we could perform—as parents, spouses, friends, lovers, teachers, students, tradespeople, civil servants, artists, intellectuals, politicians, professionals, caretakers, caring strangers. We would live conscientiously, as if our life were our work. Having been called involuntarily to life at the moment of conception, we would deliberately choose life itself as a calling. In fact, the world calls us to a life forged in bonds of love through work every instant, if only we could hear it:

Are you serious?

Are you sure?

How can you tell?

Acknowledgments

I've been writing about the nature of seriousness in American life for some time, and I would like to thank the editors at various publications who provided me with the opportunity to develop my ideas. At the *Wall Street Journal*, Mike Miller, Eben Shapiro, and Lauren Mechling gave me the freedom to examine the American suburbs, contemporary comedy, the crossroads where politics and culture meet, and the fate of portraiture in essays that made their way into these pages in different form. The editors of the *New York Times Book Review* allowed me to publish what became early versions of chapters on George Steiner, Marion Ettlinger, Freud, the affinities between the Beats and the Tea Party, and the hazards of a purely literary education. Tom Watson, Edward Felsenthal, and Tina Brown at the *Daily Beast* offered me the chance to try and figure out just how serious John Updike, Irving Kristol, and Chesley Sullenberger were, and what happened to American intellectuals in a time of economic crisis and confusion. At *Slate*, Meghan O'Rourke happily supported my musings on the ascendancy of Pixar and the rapid evolution of intelligent animation. Many of the pages on American politics, celebrity, and the novel got their start with Kyle Pope, Christopher Stewart, and the inestimable Alexandra Jacobs at the *New York Observer*. The section on Oprah first appeared in another incarnation in *The New Republic*.

I am grateful to Adam Bellow, my editor, who inspired and encouraged me and deftly guided me through the maze of work that leads to a book. His superb assistant, Kathryn Whitenight, has been indispensable. I am thankful also for Emily Walters's keen eye and careful hand. Gloria Loomis is not only the ideal agent; she is a wise, good, and loyal friend.

I am lucky to know some of the most serious people alive, whose friendships nourished me as I wrote. My deepest thanks to John Donatich, Edwin Frank, Janet Malcolm, David Rieff, Gary Rosen, Ellen Rosenbush, Kent Sepkowitz, Deborah Solomon, and Gitte and Theo Theodossi.

My wife, Christina Gillham, my son, Julian, and my daughter, Harper, are my Three Muses of Seriousness. Without them, I would be too silly for words.